# Level Up! Exploring Gamification's Impact on Research and Innovation

*Edited by Tibor Guzsvinecz*

Published in London, United Kingdom

Level Up! Exploring Gamification's Impact on Research and Innovation
http://dx.doi.org/10.5772/intechopen.1001659
Edited by Tibor Guzsvinecz

Contributors
Alexandru Predescu, Annamaria Szelinger, Francisca Escudeiro, Khaled Ouanes, Mariana Mocanu, Marta Sampaio, Márcia Campos Gouveia, Nuno Escudeiro, Omar Al-Jadaan, Omnia Ibrahim Mohamed, Paula Escudeiro, Ricardo Marcão, Tibor Guzsvinecz, Vasco Santos



First published in London, United Kingdom, 2024 by IntechOpen
IntechOpen is the global imprint of INTECHOPEN LIMITED, registered in England and Wales, registration number: 11086078, 167-169 Great Portland Street, London, W1W 5PF, United Kingdom

British Library Cataloguing-in-Publication Data
A catalogue record for this book is available from the British Library

Additional hard and PDF copies can be obtained from orders@intechopen.com

Level Up! Exploring Gamification's Impact on Research and Innovation
Edited by Tibor Guzsvinecz
p. cm.
Print ISBN 978-1-83769-529-4
Online ISBN 978-1-83769-528-7
eBook (PDF) ISBN 978-1-83769-530-0

For EU product safety concerns:
IN TECH d.o.o., Prolaz Marije Krucifikse Kozulić 3, 51000 Rijeka, Croatia,
info@intechopen.com or visit our website at intechopen.com.

# Meet the editor

Dr. Tibor Guzsvinecz obtained his Ph.D. in Information Science in 2021. His research areas are data science, gamification, human-computer interaction, spatial ability, video games, and virtual reality. He has eighty-four scientific publications to his credit. He has also edited three book projects. He received seven scholarships, one section chair award from the Institute of Electrical and Electronics Engineers (IEEE), and one best publication award at a conference. He is a member of the international organizing committee of the IEEE International Conference on Cognitive Infocommunications and the IEEE International Conference on Cognitive Aspects of Virtual Reality. He is also a member of two laboratories at the University of Pannonia, Hungary. Dr. Guzsvinecz has been an IEEE member since 2023.

# Contents

# Preface

In today's evolving world, gamification has become a transformative element that redefines traditional methods. Gamification involves applying game-like elements to non-game settings, and it has shown great promise in boosting engagement, motivation, and productivity across various fields of research. *Level Up! Exploring Gamification's Impact on Research and Innovation* thoroughly examines various aspects of gamification, presenting an in-depth look at its applications and effects in different areas.

The inspiration for this book comes from recognizing gamification's significant role in promoting creativity, collaboration, and critical thinking. Each chapter is authored by scholars as well as practitioners, and all combine empirical studies, theoretical insights, and practical examples to offer a complete understanding of gamification's influence on modern research and innovation.

Chapter 1, "Analyzing the Bibliometric Trends in Gamification Research Using the Bibliometrix R-Tool" by Tibor Guzsvinecz and Annamaria Szelinger, presents a comprehensive bibliometric analysis of research papers on gamification. Using three databases—PubMed, Scopus, and Web of Science—the authors compile and analyze a dataset of 18,389 articles after eliminating potential duplicates. They provide a detailed examination of the gamification field of research while highlighting current trends, collaborations, and research interests. Their work not only maps the existing research field regarding gamification but also presents future research directions in this dynamic and evolving field. This chapter serves as a foundational piece for the book, offering readers a comprehensive overview of the scholarly activity and trends in gamification research.

Chapter 2, "Gamification in Real-World Applications: Interactive Maps and Augmented Reality" by Alexandru Predescu and Mariana Mocanu, explores gamification when applied to real-world scenarios and emphasizes the integration of geographic information systems (GIS) and augmented reality (AR). Through a thorough examination of case studies and current research, the authors demonstrate the potential of combining game design principles with interactive technologies to create immersive experiences that significantly enhance user engagement in addressing complex problems across various domains. The chapter provides a detailed analysis of how gamification, when integrated with GIS and AR, can revolutionize fields such as education, health, and smart government.

Chapter 3, "Exploring Gamification in Luxury Tourism" by Ricardo Marcão, Vasco Santos, and Marta Sampaio, provides an overview of gamification fundamentals and using them in luxury tourism. The authors discuss how technologies like augmented reality, virtual reality, and mobile applications can be used to create immersive and interactive environments that enhance the overall travel experience. By enhancing interactivity, personalization, and customer loyalty, gamified luxury tourism experiences can shape the future of the industry.

Chapter 4, “Online and Mobile-Assisted Language Learning” by Omnia Ibrahim Mohamed and Omar Al-Jadaan, examines the transformative potential of online language classes and mobile-assisted language learning applications in reshaping language education. The authors also explore the implications of these technological advancements for language learning. Through this exploration, the authors provide readers with a deep understanding of the current state and future potential of online and mobile-assisted language learning. This chapter serves as a vital resource for educators, learners, and policymakers interested in using technology to enhance language education.

Chapter 5, “Transforming Medical and Health Sciences Education with Gamification” by Khaled Ouanes, demonstrates how AI-powered gamification can transform medical and health sciences education for both healthcare professionals and patients. The personalized approach of AI allows for tailored educational experiences, adjusting the level of difficulty and content based on individual learner needs and progress. Readers of this chapter will gain a deep understanding of how AI-powered gamification has the potential to revolutionize medical and health sciences education by making it more engaging, personalized, and effective.

Chapter 6 “Unveiling the Holistic Approach of the STEAME Teacher Facilitators Academy Project” by Paula Escudeiro, Márcia Campos Gouveia, Nuno Escudeiro, and Francisca Escudeiro, explores the transformative potential in multidisciplinary, project-based learning methodologies by emphasizing the critical roles that educators and aspiring teachers play in shaping education. The authors also present the STEAME Teacher Facilitators Academy as a beacon of innovation and progress in modern education. This chapter serves as an essential resource for those committed to advancing educational practices and outcomes, offering insights into how innovative, project-based learning can drive meaningful change.

The academic editor extends his deepest gratitude to the contributing authors for their invaluable insights and to the readers for joining us in this exploration. May this book inspire you to level up your understanding and application of gamification in your respective fields.

**Dr. Tibor Guzsvinecz**
Department of Information Technology and Its Applications,
University of Pannonia,
Zalaegerszeg, Hungary

**Chapter 1**

# Analyzing the Bibliometric Trends in Gamification Research Using the Bibliometrix R-Tool

*Tibor Guzsvinecz and Annamaria Szelinger*

## Abstract

This study presents a bibliometric analysis of research papers in the field of gamification. With the use of three different databases (PubMed, Scopus, and Web of Science), we analyzed various types of studies in this field using the statistical program package R. After removing possible duplicates, we analyzed a dataset consisting of 18,389 articles regarding gamification research. The results of our study present a detailed view of the gamification landscape, showing the current trends, collaborations, and research interests. Key themes of gamification research include serious games, motivation, and design regarding its multidisciplinary nature. The results also show that there is a need for continued collaboration across disciplines and regions to address complex challenges. Based on the results, valuable insights could be provided for scholars, practitioners, and policymakers who could be interested in this dynamic and multidisciplinary field. This bibliometric analysis provides a deeper understanding of the current state of gamification studies.

**Keywords:** academia, bibliometric analysis, collaboration, gamification, publications, research landscape

## 1. Introduction

Gamification can be defined as using game design elements in non-game contexts. While the idea of gamification was tackled in the past by creating enjoyable user interfaces [1, 2], it did not gain popularity until the 2010s [3]. The rise of cheap sensors (e.g., Microsoft Kinect) played a great role in increasing the popularity of gamification [4]. It even surpassed the boundaries of entertainment and emerged as a powerful strategy tool with applications in different areas. Gamification is now a key player in education, business, health care, and marketing. By applying game mechanics, rules, reward systems, and interactive elements, gamification takes advantage of motivating users [5]. Gamification also enhances learning experiences and employee productivity while creating innovative solutions to challenges. The main purpose of gamification is to push the user's behavior in a positive direction. In most cases it does that by forming a habit loop: elements of the environment trigger users to do certain actions, then those actions are rewarded. To motivate users there are extrinsic and intrinsic motivations. Rewards and penalties are extrinsic, and relatedness, autonomy, mastery, and purpose (RAMP) are intrinsic. These factors are important to understand to know what gamification is.

In this paper, we will explore the various applications of gamification by showing its transformative influence in various fields of research. For this goal, we will investigate the research trends regarding it using bibliometric analysis. Before conducting the investigation, however, we will present a short literature review regarding the state of gamification in various areas. Section 1.1 shows a few examples of gamification in education; Section 1.2 details the use of gamification in everyday life; Section 1.3 presents a few examples of gamification in marketing; and Section 1.4 shows a few examples of gamification in health care and rehabilitation. Our research questions will be presented in Section 1.5.

### 1.1 Education

Gamification has found significant applications in the field of education, enhancing engagement, motivation, and learning. According to Rahn, the significance of engagement within educational contexts depends on the nature of the simulation and the educational setting. He proposes that engagement becomes apparent when there is a sense of competitive team spirit, as well as active discussion and debate among team members [6]. Furthermore, the level of engagement is enhanced when students are provided with clear objectives, demanding assignments, an authentic and captivating narrative, a degree of novelty, and a diverse range of intriguing characters and roles.

Software exists as well that can gamify education. One of the most known examples is "Kahoot!" [7]. Kahoot! is a platform available on desktop and mobile that allows teachers to create quizzes, discussions, and surveys in a competitive environment. It focuses on active participation and reinforces learning with a quick feedback system. Although this tool is a computer and mobile-based application, it is mostly used in the classroom, where people are present.

In addition to "Kahoot!," another prominent example of gamification in education is Duolingo [8]. Unlike classroom-centered platforms, Duolingo is designed for independent, solitary learning. This application's purpose is to make language learning easier and more enjoyable by making it an everyday habit. It introduces short learning blocks with little new information and teaches language patterns with repetitive exercises. Users can earn points, unlock levels, and compete with friends while completing language exercises.

### 1.2 Everyday use

While educational gamification apps like Kahoot! and Duolingo have proven to be effective in enhancing learning experiences, the gamification trend extends beyond the classroom, transitioning from educational tools to those integrated into daily life.

For everyday use, several gamification apps can make various activities easier to complete. To enhance productivity and help users with ADHD, an application called Habitica can be very helpful [9]. It incorporates retro role-playing game (RPG) elements, hence making household chores, goals, and routines easier as well as more enjoyable. The completion of tasks within the application rewards users with gold, experience points, and items that can be used in the game. Additionally, it incorporates a leveling system and features collectible items to further enhance user involvement. Habitica also encourages users to cooperate with their friends.

GPS services and applications have become an integral part of everyday life, serving as essential tools for travel and navigation. Waze is primarily a navigation application, and it incorporates gamification elements by allowing users to earn points, compete for achievements and badges, and participate in community challenges based on their driving behavior [10]. It also encourages users to submit travel times and route details.

The primary goal of Waze is to provide users with real-time traffic information. Although other apps encourage people to explore their surroundings not simply just travel through areas. Pokémon GO is an augmented reality game, but at the same time, it encourages players to go outside [11, 12]. For example, one aspect of the game is to hatch eggs based on walked kilometers.

Another aspect of our daily lives is paying for something. Throughout the years, mobile payment has become easier. One of the mobile payment services is Google Pay, which incorporated gamification elements in India during the 2019 Diwali season [13, 14]. Participants needed to gather at least five different types of stamps. Successfully collecting them rewarded the user 251 INR (around 3 USD), along with the opportunity to win 1 INR Lakh (around 1207 USD). These stamps could be collected through various actions in the application: spending a certain amount, requesting a friend for a stamp, sharing a stamp, and many more actions.

### 1.3 Marketing

In marketing, consumer engagement is very important as well as brand loyalty. To achieve this, gamification emerged as a powerful tool and transformed the way businesses interact with their audience. With collectible badges, points, and rewards, companies motivate people to consume and use their products more frequently. Fast food restaurants around the world, such as McDonald's, KFC, and Burger King have similar applications, where users can earn points or rewards for making purchases through them [15].

Gamification in marketing focuses on loyalty programs, interactive quizzes, and surveys. Mobile applications with rewards, referral programs, and social media challenges are also observable. While real-life gamification is rare in marketing, "Decoded," Jay-Z's memoir book employed an innovative marketing campaign that included gamification [16]. The campaign featured a digital scavenger hunt where pages of the book were hidden in various locations. By doing so, this campaign challenged fans to decode the clues and discover the hidden content. The scavenger hunt had both online and offline components. The gamification aspect added an element of excitement and exploration to the traditional book launch.

Marketing extends widely across all fields and industries, encompassing hospitality as well. One example of a marketing strategy that includes gamification is the Marriott Bonvoy, which is the loyalty program of the Marriott Hotels chain [17]. It applies a point-based system that rewards members for their interactions with the hotel chain. Interactions not only include hotel stays but also dining in restaurants or interacting with the brand through social media. By participating in the program, guests can have tiered memberships, and consequently, they can unlock exclusive perks, room upgrades, and access to special events.

Mariott Hotels also launched a game application for Facebook, a virtual simulation that allowed players to experience various aspects of running a Marriott hotel as the hotel manager [18]. The game's goal was to promote careers in hospitality and to attract the workforce to the Marriott Hotels.

### 1.4 Health care and rehabilitation

In health care and rehabilitation, gamification apps have a transformative approach to patient engagement and recovery. The applications in health care can be categorized mainly into four categories: physical fitness, medication, and chronic condition management; solutions aimed at children; physical therapy; and rehabilitation. Gamification can also encourage people to engage in physical exercise and make fitness routines more enjoyable, at the same time can also help medical students, residents, and staff to learn [19, 20].

A validated laparoscopic serious game, Underground was developed to enhance laparoscopic skills training [21]. The game utilizes a virtual environment to simulate laparoscopic procedures, allowing users to practice and refine their skills in a risk-free setting. Underground incorporates game elements to make the learning and exercising process more enjoyable. There is also a storyline besides challenges, scenarios, and rewards creating an immersive environment. Underground seeks to overcome the barriers that may limit residents' voluntary engagement in training activities.

In the case of people living with diseases and health problems, gamification can make everyday life easier and can effectively help them learn new habits to maintain their health regardless of their condition. Especially children need to learn at a young age how to live and protect their health with their conditions. One such serious game is called El Mundo de Celia [22]. The game aims to teach children with celiac disease to what is the disease they have, what are the symptoms, and what can they eat. The main character, Celia's objective is to maintain her health by overcoming challenges, with each successful task rewarded with points and potential life restoration. The gameplay involves interactive elements and audiovisual aids, with characters providing instructions and reinforcement messages. However, there are numerous other serious games similar to this one, which can assist children in adopting healthy dietary habits and adapting to their condition.

At the same time, gamification can help with rehabilitation. While the patient focuses on a task, they experience less pain, and they are much more willing to do the exercises. Articares developed a portable arm rehabilitation robot called H-Man used for serious games [23]. The robot consists of a modular handle and a display. It autonomously adjusts to the user's performance, continually assessing movements and modifying exercise complexity to optimize learning and offer real-time feedback on recovery progress. H-Man includes a range of games, such as exploring a virtual world, flying drones, matching hidden objects, and fishing. Similarly, the use of cheap sensors with the help of applications using gamification elements can assist in the physical rehabilitation of patients, even at their homes: according to studies in the literature, multiple algorithms were developed for this goal, mainly to maintain the motivations of patients during the rehabilitation process [24, 25].

### 1.5 Research questions

Throughout our introduction, we explored the concept of gamification and its widespread applications across various domains. From educational platforms to navigation apps, marketing, and payment services, gamification has become an integral aspect of numerous fields. By integrating gamification elements into non-gaming contexts, such as points, badges, challenges, and social features, these platforms seek to enhance engagement, motivation, and learning while transforming routine activities into interactive and rewarding experiences. Overall, gamification stands as a potential tool to revolutionize engagement, learning, and behavior change, transforming routine tasks into engaging activities across a spectrum of fields and applications.

As can be observed, however, the application of gamification elements is vast. Therefore, it is critical to understand the use of gamification in scientific studies. In light of the expansive reach of gamification, this study aims to provide a comprehensive understanding of its literature by addressing how and when such studies were conducted. To understand this, a bibliometric analysis is needed which is a quantitative method to analyze several aspects of scientific literature [26–28]. Similarly to the increasing popularity of gamification, the popularity of bibliometric analysis has increased through the years. This method is used to uncover collaboration patterns and emerging trends and to understand how a certain domain is structured in the scientific literature [29–31]. Thus, with bibliometric analysis, the goal of this chapter is to understand how gamification research is conducted. Therefore, five research questions (RQs) were formed:

- RQ1: How does the trend of gamification research papers change through the years?
- RQ2: Which countries and institutions are prominent in gamification research?
- RQ3: What countries and institutions exhibit the highest levels of collaboration in gamification research?
- RQ4: What are the main themes in such research papers?
- RQ5: What are the most frequently occurring words in gamification studies?

By addressing these five research questions, we can understand the bibliometric trends of gamification studies. With the first research question, we aim to analyze the temporal evolution of gamification literature. By examining the publication trends over time, we can understand patterns of growth and fluctuations in gamification research. Understanding these temporal dynamics provides insights into the evolving interest and attention toward gamification across different periods. With the second research question, we seek to identify the geographical distribution and institutional affiliations contributing to gamification research. By analyzing the origins of published papers, we can determine the global prominence and concentration of research activity in gamification. Moreover, this analysis may reveal potential geographic or institutional clusters of expertise and collaboration networks within the field. In the case of the third research question, the focus is on exploring collaborative patterns among countries and institutions engaged in gamification research. Understanding the dynamics of collaboration can shed light on knowledge exchange, interdisciplinary interactions, and the formation of research networks driving gamification scholarship. With the fourth research question, we aim to identify recurring topics, concepts, and research themes explored in published papers. Through analyzing the abstracts, we can characterize the range of subjects addressed in gamification research. By identifying dominant themes, we can gain insights into the key areas of focus, emerging trends, and research priorities within the field. Lastly, in the case of the fifth research question, we aim to identify the most commonly occurring words, phrases, or terms across the papers. This analysis provides insights into the language and terminology employed by scholars in discussing concepts of gamification.

This chapter is structured as follows. First, the materials and methods are presented in Section 2, focusing on the data collection and analysis aspects of this study. Next, the results of the data analysis are presented in Section 3 of this book chapter. Afterward, the results are discussed in Section 4. Lastly, conclusions are drawn in Section 5.

## 2. Materials and methods

This section is split into three sections. Section 2.1 presents the data collection process from various scientific databases. Afterward, data analysis is detailed in Section 2.2.

### 2.1 Data collection

Data collection was conducted on September 3, 2023, using three databases: PubMed Central, Scopus, and Web of Science. The following phrase was used when searching for articles regarding gamification: "gamification" OR "gamify" OR "gamified" OR "game element." 1808, 15,820, and 9497 articles were found in these three databases, respectively. This means a total of 27,125 articles. The abstracts and keywords of these articles were downloaded via the Web sites of these databases. The files of each database were imported into the statistical program package R with the *convert2df* function found in the *bibliometrix* package [32]. Besides importing, this function also creates bibliographic data frames in R.

R is a free and open-source programming language and software environment specifically designed for statistical computing and graphics. It is widely used by statisticians, data scientists, researchers, and analysts for data analysis, visualization, and modeling tasks. It offers powerful tools for manipulating data, including functions for data cleaning, transformation, subsetting, merging, and reshaping, among others. Its functionality can be extended through the use of other packages, which are collections of R functions, data, and documentation. There are thousands of packages available for various purposes. Such a package is the aforementioned *bibliometrix* package that was used for this research. Originally, it was a console application, but it was given a graphical user interface with the help of RStudio. This graphical user interface is shown in **Figure 1**. Overall, R is a versatile tool used for data analysis, and it is also widely used in scientific research as well as in bibliometric analysis [33–40].

### 2.2 Data analysis

Firstly, using the previously mentioned *convert2df* function, three data frames were created, one for each scientific database. Once the data regarding gamification research were downloaded and imported into R, the data preprocessing phase commenced. Preprocessing was necessary before analysis since there could be duplicates in the 27,125 articles. Removing duplicates was done with the *mergeDbSources* function. With this function, 8736 duplicates were removed from the data frame, resulting in 18,389 articles. To check whether there were still some duplicates in the data frame, the *duplicatedMatching* function was used with its default values. With them, this function uses the restricted Damerau-Levenshtein distance to find duplicated articles

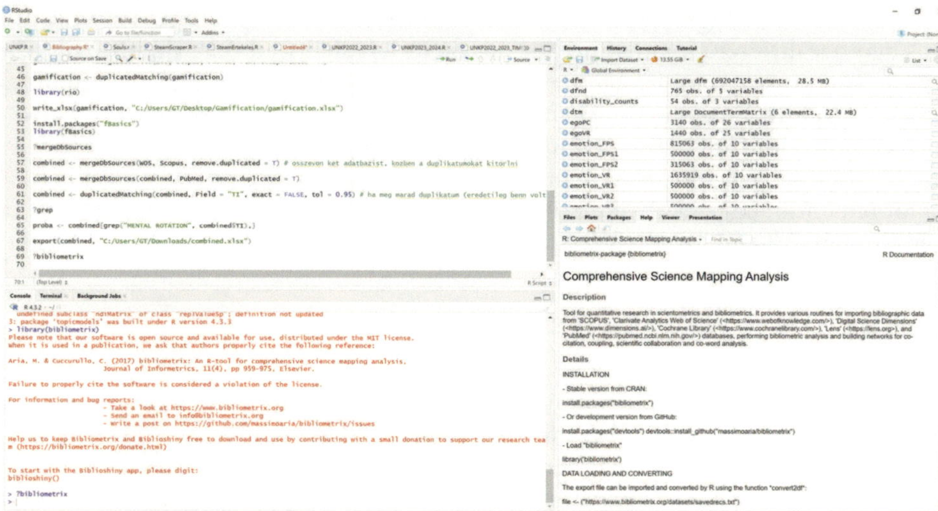

**Figure 1.**
*Graphical user interface of R studio. Upper left window: This is where the users can write code. Lower left window: the console in which the results are yielded. Upper right window: the used variables (e.g., vectors and matrices) in the current environment. Lower right window: at the moment, the documentation of the used package.*

with at least 0.95 minimum relative similarity between their title fields. However, no other duplicates were found in the data frame. Therefore, the previously mentioned data frame of 18,389 articles was used for further investigation.

For the investigation, the *biblioshiny* function was used. As with the previously mentioned functions, this one can also be found in the *bibliometrix* package. This function provides an intuitive graphical user interface for investigating bibliographic data. A screenshot of this interface can be seen in **Figure 2**. This interface can be invoked with the use of the *biblioshiny* function in R.

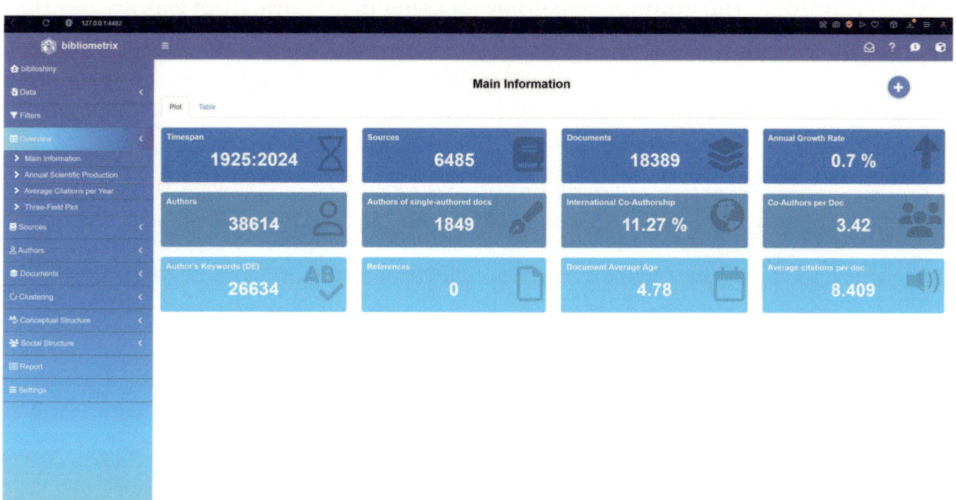


**Figure 2.**
*Screenshot of the bibliometrix package. It also provides the general results of the analysis.*

As can be seen in **Figure 2**, the interface of the *bibliometrix* package is quite intuitive. There are different menus and buttons on its left side, and they simply had to be pressed. By doing so, the package automatically did the data analysis of the imported dataset. Therefore, by using this interface, data summaries and plots can be created with a click of a button. In this chapter, all plots (except for **Figure 15**) were created with this package. For the creation of **Figure 15**, the *ggplot2* package was used in R. This aforementioned package contains functions for better visualization. For clustering in Sections 3.3 and 3.4, the Walktrap algorithm was used in this package as well.

## 3. Results

The 18,389 investigated documents consist of the following. Out of these, 7445 are articles, 117 are books, 4968 are conference papers, 554 are conference reviews, 146 are editorial materials, 3315 are proceedings papers, and 727 are reviews. The remaining 1117 are other types of documents such as letters, surveys, corrections, and data papers. 26,634 keywords were used overall in the investigated studies. The average age of the documents was 4.78. Regarding authors, their number in the data frame is 38,614. While the number of co-authors per document is 3.42 on average, only 1849 articles are written by a single author. The percentage of international co-authorship is 11.27%. Regarding citations, their average is 8.40 per document.

To examine these numbers in more detail, this section is split into five sections. Each section presents the results regarding each research question.

### 3.1 Annual scientific research on gamification

First, to understand the number of gamification papers in the literature, the annual publication information was investigated. The results are illustrated in **Figure 3**.

The first found research on gamification dates back to 1925. After that, little to no research was conducted until the 2000s when gamification started to gain popularity. Starting from 2008, the number of studies focusing on gamification was greater than

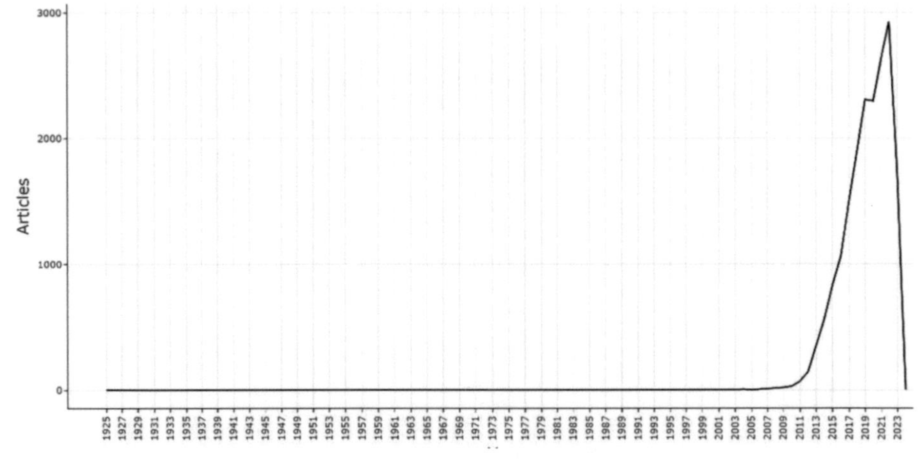


**Figure 3.**
*Annual scientific research on gamification between 1925 and 2023.*

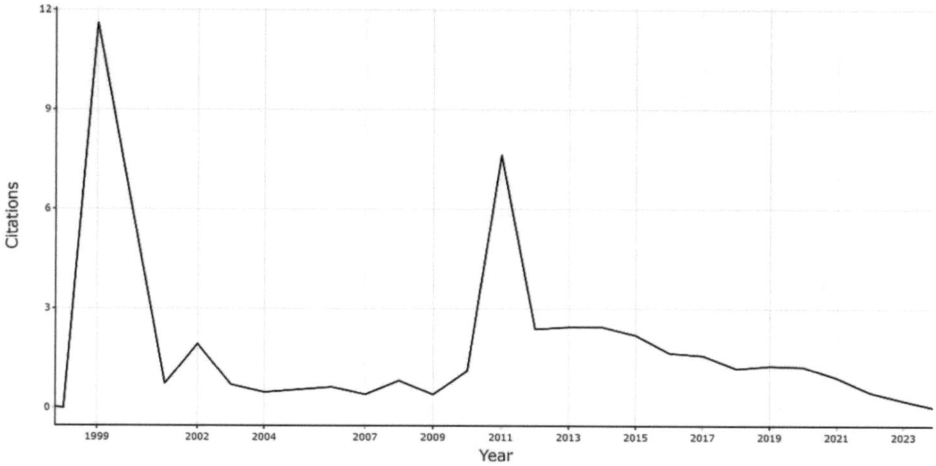


**Figure 4.**
*Average number of citations per year.*

10. In 2012, the number of such studies became greater than 100, with 144 research papers. In 2016 the number of gamification studies was larger than 1000, with 1058 publications. Similarly, starting in 2019, the number of studies became greater than 2000 per year. In 2022, the number of published papers in the investigated datasets was 2927. Only 1710 studies were found in 2013, although the year was not yet over when this bibliometric analysis was conducted.

Afterward, the average number of citations was assessed throughout the years. They are shown in **Figure 4**.

As can be observed in **Figure 4**, the largest average number of citations can be found in 1999 with 11.62 citations. Soon after, this average number started to decline. However, it increased in 2011 to 7.64 per year. Afterward, it slowly decreased again. This is due to the increasing number of publications regarding gamification. As their number increases, the citations become more widespread among them.

### 3.2 Most relevant countries and institutions in gamification research

The most relevant countries in gamification research were the next to be investigated. Countries and articles were calculated based on the affiliation of the corresponding authors. The results of the analysis can be observed in **Figure 5**. Also, two abbreviations are present in the figure: multiple country publications (MCP) and single country publications (SCP).

The largest number of gamification articles are from the USA (1131); however, Spain is a close second (1120). Their rates of inter-country and intra-country publications are also very similar to each other. They are 0.132 and 0.131, respectively. The third largest number of gamification articles belongs to China (607), and its ratio of inter-country and intra-country is 0.211.

Next, the citations of these countries were assessed. The results of the analysis are shown in **Figure 6**.

Regarding citations, the USA was the most cited country in gamification research with 15,500 citations. The next one was Spain with 8379, and China was the third with 6711 citations. As can be seen in **Figures 5** and **6**, the first three countries were the same ones in both cases. Afterward, their order changed drastically.

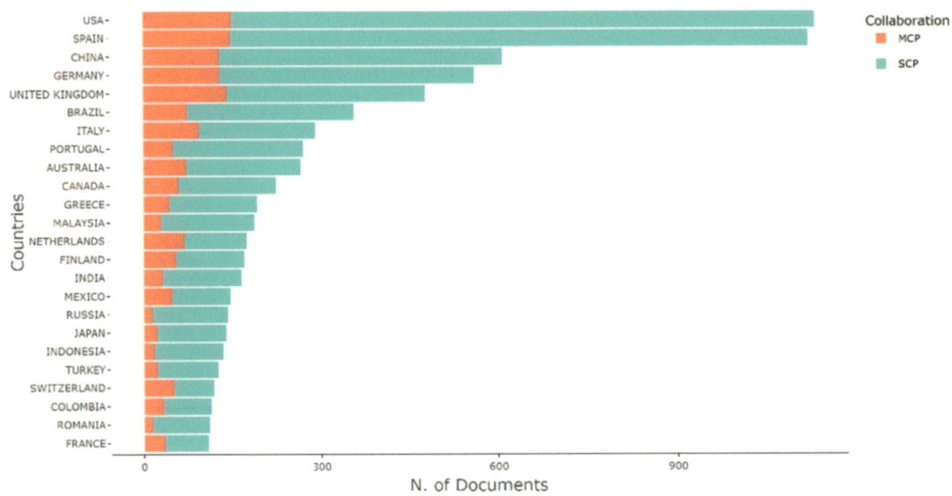


**Figure 5.**
*25 most relevant countries in gamification research.*

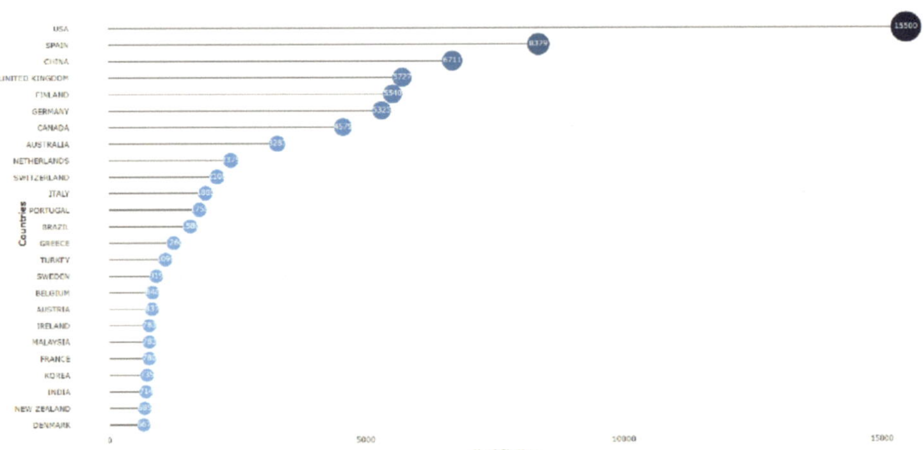


**Figure 6.**
*25 most cited countries in gamification research.*

The next step was to assess the average number of citations of countries. The results are shown in **Figure 7**.

Compared to **Figures 5** and **6**, the order of countries is completely different when their average number of citations was investigated. Here, the first three most averagely cited countries are Finland, Canada, and Morocco, with 32.8, 20.5, and 20.3 citations, respectively.

To better understand where these documents were created, the various institutions were investigated next. The results of the investigation can be seen in **Figure 8**.

Even though the largest number of gamification research papers come from the USA, **Figure 8** shows that the largest number of articles are written by a Spanish university. University of Granada (or Univ Granada as seen in scientific databases) has written 182 articles regarding gamification. With 143 documents, the second place belongs to a Portuguese university: the University of Porto (Univ Porto). The third,

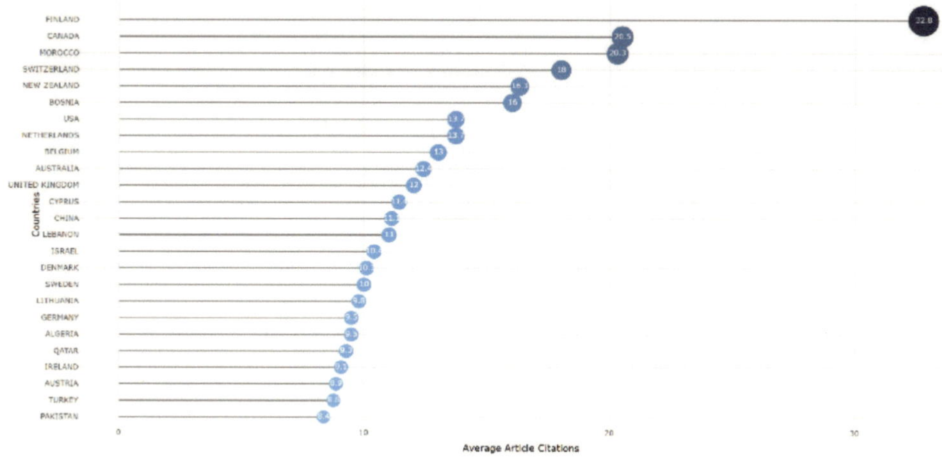


**Figure 7.**
*25 most averagely cited countries in gamification research.*

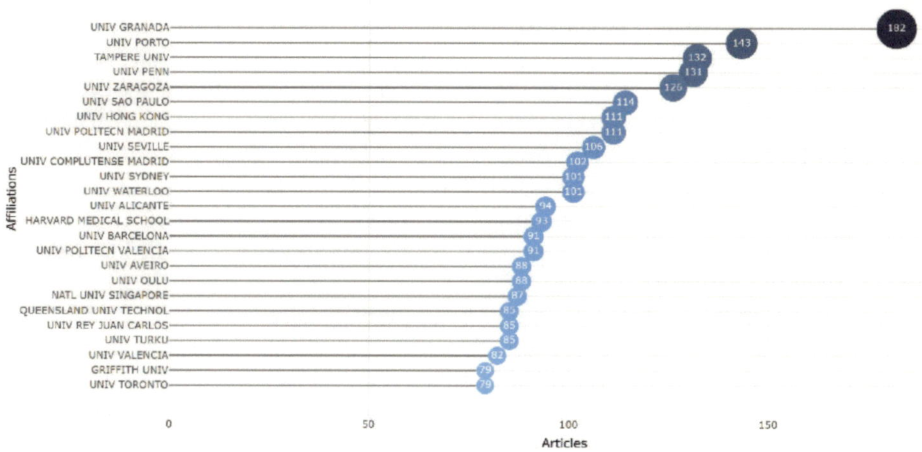


**Figure 8.**
*25 most relevant institutions in gamification research.*

with 132 documents, is Tampere University from Finland. The fourth affiliation is from the USA, the University of Pennsylvania.

Overall, 12 affiliations have written over 100 documents related to gamification. 53 affiliations have written at least 50 research papers in this field. However, 6969 affiliations have written less than 50 studies about gamification. Out of these, 6301 have written less than 10 documents in this field. The number of those affiliations that have written less than 5 studies is 5580. This fact suggests gamification is not the main profile of a large number of affiliations, or that they just started researching in this field.

### 3.3 Collaboration between countries and institutions

The following to investigate was the collaboration between countries. The results of the analyses are shown in **Figure 9**.

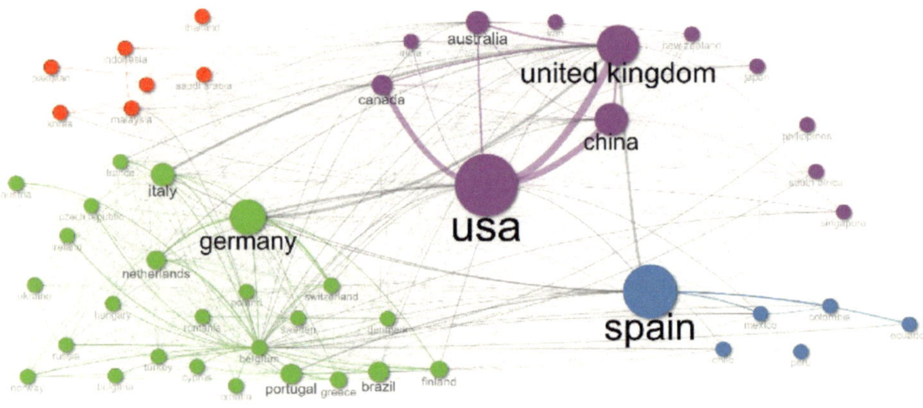


**Figure 9.**
*Collaboration between countries.*

Based on node color and size, it is possible to determine which countries frequently collaborate. The USA mainly collaborates with the United Kingdom, China, Australia, Iran, New Zealand, Singapore, Japan, South Africa, and the Philippines. It also collaborates—albeit less frequently—with Spain and other countries. Looking at the green color, it can be said that the European countries mainly collaborate with each other, with Spain being an exception. Spain frequently collaborates with Mexico, Colombia, Chile, Peru, and Ecuador. Some Asian and Middle-Eastern countries also frequently collaborate with each other: Thailand, Saudi Arabia, United Arab Emirates, Indonesia, Malaysia, Korea, and Pakistan.

Similarly, the collaboration between institutions was assessed as well. The results can be observed in **Figure 10**.

According to **Figure 10**, some universities frequently collaborate with each other. One of the largest collaborators is Tampere University which collaborates with the University of Waterloo, the University of Sao Paulo, the University of Turku, the University of Oulu, and the University of Toronto. This indicates a large collaboration between Finland and Canada. Another large collaborator is the University of Granada. It collaborates with the University of Alicante, the University of Salamanca,

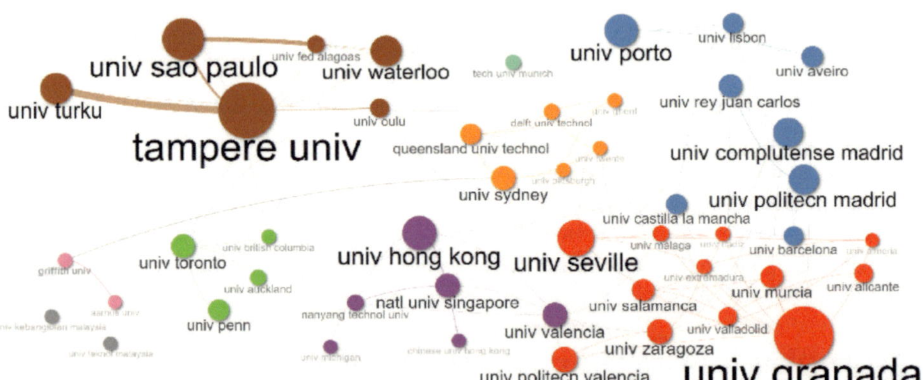


**Figure 10.**
*Collaboration between institutions.*

the University of Valladolid, the University of Murcia, the University of Seville, and the University of Almeria. This indicates a collaboration between Spanish universities. However, all have smaller collaborations with multiple universities from other countries. As can be seen in **Figure 10**, there are other collaborating universities as well, although they collaborate less frequently with each other.

### 3.4 Themes in gamification research

To understand gamification research, the themes of such papers were analyzed. The results are presented in **Figure 11**. They can be found in the form of a co-occurrence network.

Naturally, the main theme of such studies is gamification. However, the themes are closely connected to each other. Serious games, motivation, design, game, education, learning, mobile applications, human(s), health, and video games are closely related. Similarly, students, computer games, behavioral research, artificial intelligence, learning systems, game-based learning, game elements, augmented reality, virtual reality, surveys, game design, software design, education computing, information use, information systems, human-computer interaction, teaching, e-learning, curricula, engineering education, and computer-aided instruction are also closely related. Also, classroom, management, impact, self-determination theory, model, satisfaction, games, intrinsic motivation, performance, engagement, framework, technology, and behavior are closely related.

Judging from the themes in gamification studies, the following can be observed. There are three main categories of themes, centering around gamification elements. The first is about serious games which can be created for multiple purposes. The second is about design elements in such contexts. Lastly, the third is about the gamified environment and its impact on users.

### 3.5 Words in gamification research

To better understand the themes in papers related to gamification, the words in their abstracts were investigated. Firstly, the investigation continued with unigrams. The results of the analysis can be observed in **Figure 12**.

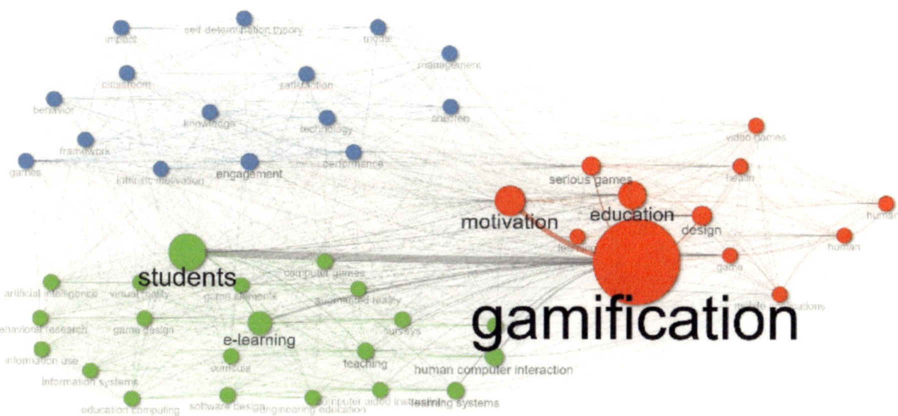


**Figure 11.**
*Co-occurrence network of themes in gamification research.*

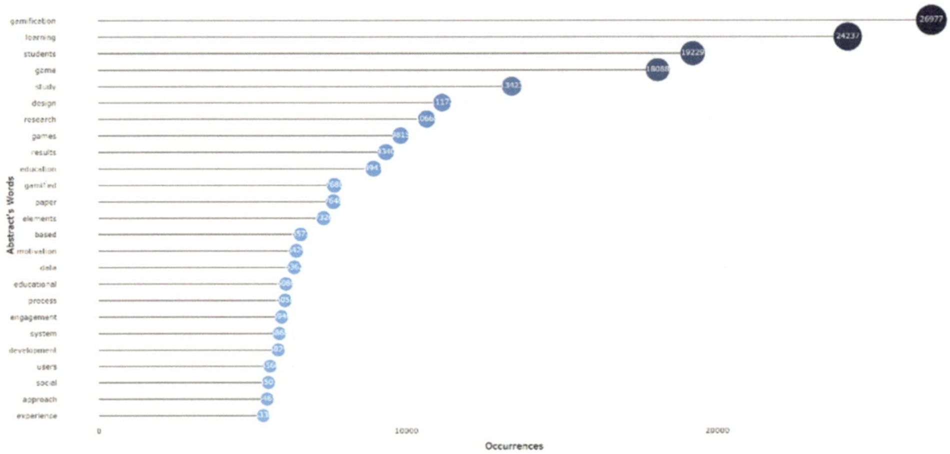


**Figure 12.**
*25 most common unigrams in the abstracts of gamification studies.*

When looking at the 25 most common unigrams in the abstracts, the following can be concluded. The most common word is gamification with 26,977 occurrences, followed by learning and students, with 24,237 and 19,229 respective occurrences. Game (18,088), study (13,423), and design (11,172) are also common, indicating some themes of the research. Common words also include motivation (6429), educational (6080), and engagement (5948).

However, to better understand the contents of the investigated research papers about gamification, the investigation continued with bigrams. The results are shown in **Figure 13**.

Regarding bigrams, the most common was "game elements" with 2613 occurrences. This was followed by "game design," "gamification elements," "virtual reality," and "learning process" with 1443, 1195, 1112, and 1078 occurrences, respectively. "Game-based learning" (1059), "game mechanics" (740), "user experience" (704), "intrinsic motivation" (609), and "learning experience" (552) were also frequent.

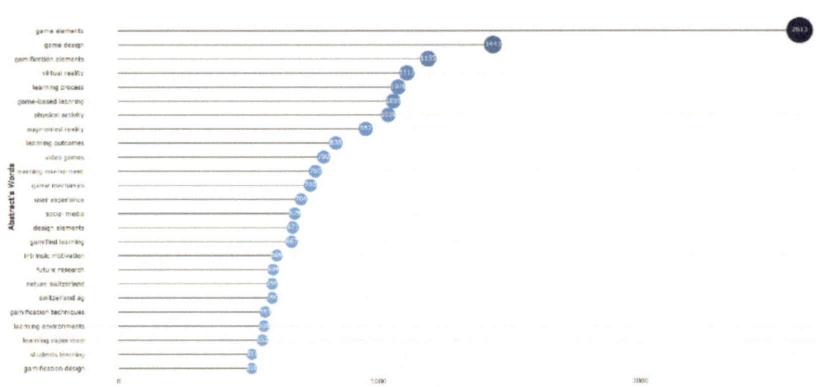


**Figure 13.**
*25 most common bigrams in the abstracts of gamification studies.*

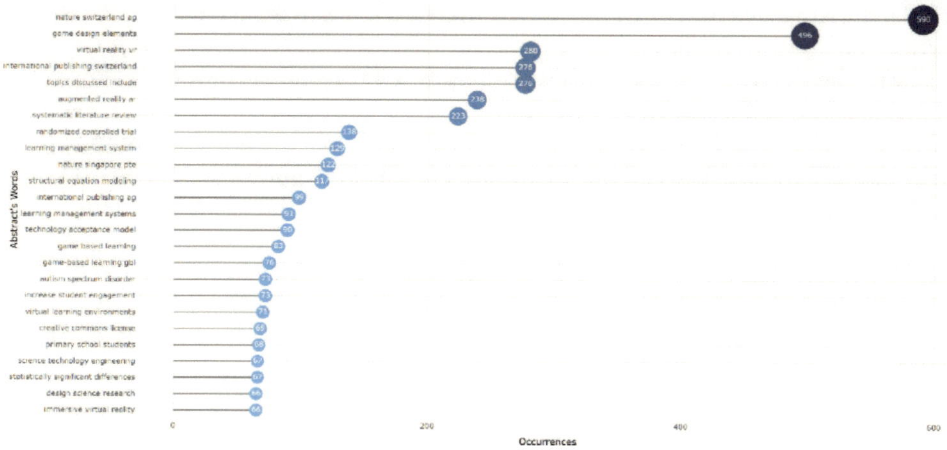


**Figure 14.**
*25 most common trigrams in the abstracts of gamification studies.*

Next, trigrams were assessed. The results of the assessment can be observed in **Figure 14**.

Regarding trigrams, "game design elements," "virtual reality vr," "augmented reality vr," "systematic literature review," and "randomized controlled trial" were frequent with a respective occurrence of 496, 280, 238, 223, and 138. Other trigrams

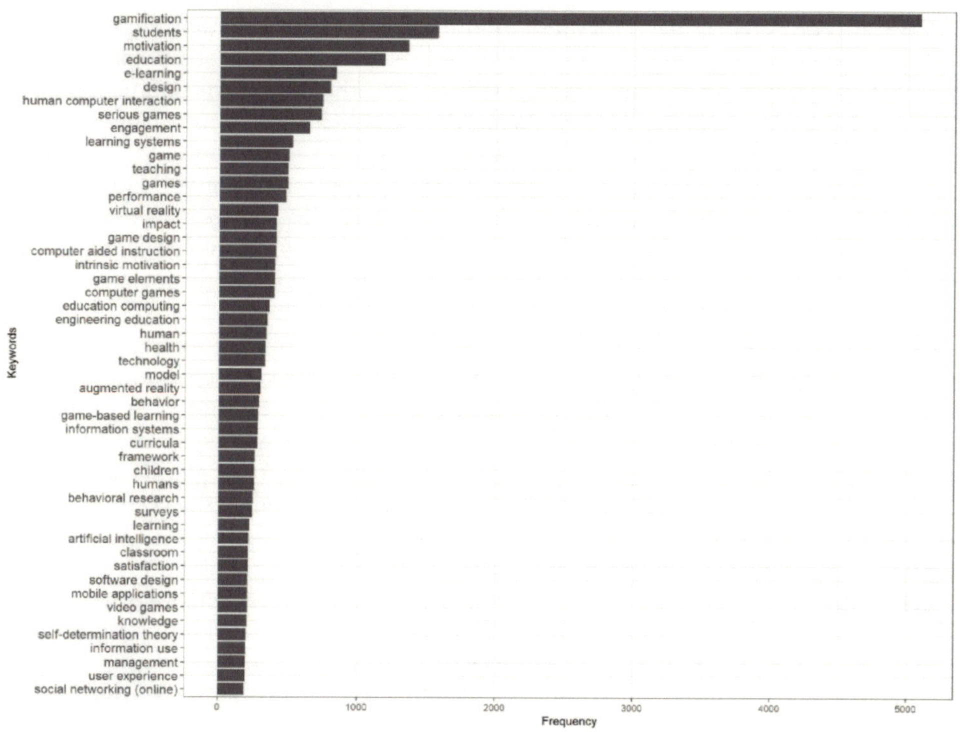


**Figure 15.**
*Most common keywords in gamification research.*

include "autism spectrum disorder" (73), "increase student engagement" (73), and "virtual learning environments" (71).

Lastly, the keywords of the studies were assessed. The most common keywords can be observed in **Figure 15**.

It can be observed in **Figure 15** that "gamification" was the most common keyword with 5094 occurrences. This means 20% of all investigated documents. The next keyword was students, with 1572 occurrences (6% of the investigated documents). Afterward, motivation and education were the most common with 1362 and 1187 occurrences, respectively. Both keywords could be found in around 5% of the investigated documents. They were followed by e-learning (843), design (801), human-computer interaction (746), serious games (735), and engagement (650). The occurrences of the other keywords were 2% at most.

## 4. Discussion

A bibliometric analysis holds significant importance in academic research. It provides a quantitative assessment of scholarly output within a particular field or discipline. By analyzing publication data, citations, and other bibliographic indicators, it is possible to gain insights into trends and the impact of research outputs over time. It is also possible to map collaboration networks among researchers, institutions, and countries. By analyzing co-authorship patterns and collaboration networks, researchers can identify key collaborators, research clusters, and interdisciplinary connections. This information is valuable for fostering collaboration, promoting knowledge exchange, and enhancing research productivity.

Naturally, like any research method, bibliometric analysis has its strengths and limitations. Its accuracy depends on various factors. The accuracy of bibliometric analysis also depends on the comprehensiveness and coverage of the database used. Different databases may have varying coverage of publications across different disciplines, languages, and regions. Incomplete or biased coverage can limit the accuracy of the analysis, particularly when drawing conclusions about the investigated field of research. Also, bibliometric data are dynamic and subject to change over time. New publications are constantly being added, and citation counts can evolve as research progresses. Updates to the dataset are necessary to maintain the accuracy of bibliometric analysis over time.

However, it is possible to understand what the field of gamification research looks like at this current moment. According to the results, the research questions were answered. Regarding RQ1, the following can be stated. There has been a large increase in the number of gamification research papers over the years, particularly from the 2000s onwards. This rise coincides with the growing popularity of gamification as a research topic. Notably, starting from 2012, there has been a substantial surge since the number of studies exceeded 1000 per year by 2016. This exponential growth suggests a heightened interest and recognition of the importance of gamification in various domains. The average number of citations per year provides additional insight, showing fluctuations over time. The peak in 1999 followed by a decline could be attributed to the nascent stage of gamification research. Here, the seminal works might have garnered initial attention. Subsequent fluctuations reflect the dynamic nature of research trends and the increasing number of publications.

Regarding RQ2, the following can be stated. The USA emerges as a main contributor to gamification research in terms of both the number of publications and citations.

However, Spain and China also demonstrate significant activity, with Spain particularly notable for its high citation rate relative to publication count. This suggests the high quality and impact of research that originates from Spain. The analysis of institutions reveals several contributors: the University of Granada, the University of Porto, and Tampere University can be found among the leaders. While the USA leads in overall output, individual institutions from Spain, Portugal, and Finland demonstrate notable engagement and productivity in gamification research.

In the case of RQ3, the results implicate the following. Collaboration between countries and institutions plays a significant role in advancing gamification research. The analysis highlights patterns of collaboration, with the USA engaging in extensive international partnerships, particularly with European and Asian countries. Spain emerges as an active collaborator with mainly Latin American nations. These facts indicate regional research networks. Among institutions, Tampere University stands out for its large number of collaborations. It also has connections with universities across different countries. Similarly, the University of Granada demonstrates a strong network of collaboration within Spain and other countries. This showcases the importance of institutional partnerships in advancing gamification research.

The results of RQ4 shows that there are several key areas of focus within gamification research. These areas include serious games, motivation, design, education, and learning. These themes intersect and contribute to a holistic understanding of gamification's applications and implications across various domains. The emphasis on educational contexts shows the complex nature of gamification research.

Similarly, the results of RQ5 present the frequent words in gamification research. The frequency of terms such as "gamification," "learning," "students," and "motivation" reflects dominant themes and areas of interest. Bigrams and trigrams provide additional information that highlights specific combinations of words that recurrently appear in research papers, such as "game elements," "virtual reality," and "game-based learning."

Consequently, the importance of the results offers valuable insights into various aspects of this vast field. By tracking the annual publication count and citation trends, researchers, policymakers, and practitioners can gain a comprehensive understanding of the trajectory of gamification research. This awareness allows them to anticipate emerging trends, identify gaps in knowledge, and allocate resources. The analysis of collaboration between countries and institutions presents the global nature of gamification research. Collaborations can exchange diverse perspectives, methodologies, and expertise. This can enrich the research landscape about gamification. Such collaborations can also promote the dissemination of best practices and innovative approaches. The identification of countries and institutions in gamification research serves multiple purposes. First, it provides recognition for the contributions of leading researchers and institutions. Additionally, it helps aspiring researchers and institutions identify potential collaborators and mentors. This could allow for mentorship and knowledge transfer within the academic community. Thematic analysis reveals the primary areas of focus within gamification research. This could guide researchers in making informed decisions regarding research priorities, resource allocation, and strategic initiatives.

Overall, the insights gained from gamification research have practical implications for various sectors, including education, health care, marketing, and research. Effective design principles can enable researchers to develop more engaging and effective applications. For educators, gamification principles can enhance student engagement, motivation, and learning outcomes, leading to more effective pedagogical practices. Policymakers can also gain insights from gamification research to inform the development of frameworks and guidelines regarding its ethical use.

## 5. Conclusions

The findings of this study shed light on the trajectory, global distribution, collaborative networks, thematic focus, and prevalent terminology within the research areas of gamification. Understanding these aspects is essential for appreciating the significance and implications of gamification in various domains.

Regarding the results, the following could be stated. First, the interest in gamification research papers increased throughout the years. This increase shows the need for continued exploration of gamification elements and applications. Second, the involvement of countries such as the USA, Spain, and China in gamification research highlights its global relevance and the diversity of perspectives contributing to its development. Collaborative networks play a pivotal role in fostering knowledge exchange and innovation in this dynamic field. Third, the identification of key themes such as serious games, motivation, and design presents the multidisciplinary nature of gamification research. As was mentioned, these themes intersect with various disciplines, including education, health care, and business, emphasizing the multidisciplinary nature of gamification and its potential to address complex challenges. Fourth, by understanding the prevalent themes and terminology within gamification research, researchers can design more effective gamified environments, policies, and strategies for their desired outcomes.

As gamification continues to evolve, future research directions may include exploring emerging technologies (e.g., virtual reality and augmented reality), assessing the long-term impacts of gamified environments, and investigating cultural variations in gamification. Additionally, there is a need for continued collaboration across disciplines and regions to address complex challenges. In conclusion, the results presented in this study contribute to a deeper understanding of gamification research and its implications. By leveraging these insights, researchers can enhance user engagement, motivation, and learning outcomes across diverse contexts.

## Acknowledgements

This work has been implemented by the TKP2021-NVA-10 project with the support provided by the Ministry of Culture and Innovation of Hungary from the National Research, Development and Innovation Fund, financed under the 2021 Thematic Excellence Programme funding scheme.

## Conflict of interest

The authors declare no conflict of interest.

## Author details

Tibor Guzsvinecz* and Annamaria Szelinger
Faculty of Information Technology, Department of Information Technology and Its Applications, University of Pannonia, Zalaegerszeg, Hungary

*Address all correspondence to: guzsvinecz.tibor@zek.uni-pannon.hu

## References

[1] Malone TW. What makes things fun to learn? Heuristics for designing instructional computer games. In: Proceedings of the 3rd ACM SIGSMALL Symposium and the First SIGPC Symposium on Small Systems—SIGSMALL '80. New York, USA: ACM Press; 1980. pp. 162-169. DOI: 10.1145/800088.802839

[2] Malone TW. Heuristics for designing enjoyable user interfaces: Lessons from computer games. In: Proc 1982 Conference on Human Factors in Computing Systems. New York, NY, USA: ACM Press; 1982. pp. 63-68. DOI: 10.1145/800049.801756

[3] Gamification—Explore—Google Trends [Internet]. 2023. Available from: https://trends.google.com/trends/explore?date=all&q=gamification [Accessed: September 3, 2023]

[4] Deterding S. Gamification: Designing for motivation. Interactions. 2012;**19**(4):14-17. DOI: 10.1145/2212877.2212883

[5] Landers RN, Auer EM, Collmus AB, Armstrong MB. Gamification science, its history and future: Definitions and a research agenda. Simulation and Gaming. 2018;**49**(3):315-337. DOI: 10.1177/1046878118774385

[6] Rahn D. Enhancing web-based simulations with game elements for increased engagement. Business Simulation and Experiential Learning. 2009;**36**:303-311

[7] Bicen H, Kocakoyun S. Perceptions of students for gamification approach: Kahoot as a case study. International Journal of Emerging Technologies in Learning. 2018;**13**(02):72. DOI: 10.3991/ijet.v13i02.7467

[8] Huynh D, Zuo L, Iida H. Analyzing gamification of "duolingo" with focus on its course structure. In: Lecture Notes in Computer Science. Cham: Springer International Publishing; 2016. pp. 268-277

[9] Diefenbach S, Müssig A. Counterproductive effects of gamification: An analysis on the example of the gamified task manager Habitica. International Journal of Human Computer Studies. 2019;**127**:190-210. DOI: 10.1016/j.ijhcs.2018.09.004

[10] Kim B. The popularity of gamification in the mobile and social era. Library Technology Reports. 2015;**51**(2):5-9

[11] Guo Y, Peeta S, Agrawal S, Benedyk I. Impacts of Pokémon GO on route and mode choice decisions: Exploring the potential for integrating augmented reality, gamification, and social components in mobile apps to influence travel decisions. Transportation (Amst). 2022;**49**(2):395-444. DOI: 10.1007/s11116-021-10181-9

[12] Yang CC, Sia WY, Tseng YC, Chiu JC. Gamification of learning in tourism industry: A case study of Pokémon Go. In: Proceedings of the 2018 2nd International Conference on Education and E-Learning. New York; NY, USA: ACM; 2018. pp. 191-195. DOI: 10.1145/3291078.3291113

[13] Pednekar N. Is gamification the future of advertising? Results of case analysis in Indian and American Markets. In: Весенние Дни Науки: Сборник Докладов Международной Конференции Студентов и Молодых Ученых-Екатеринбург, 2023. Yekaterinburg,

Russia: УрФУ (Ural Federal University); 2023. pp. 754-756

[14] Ranjan A. GooglePay's Gamification Strategy—Diwali Stamps Collection [Internet]. Linkedin.com. 2019. Available from: https://www.linkedin.com/pulse/googlepays-gamification-strategy-diwali-stamps-arpit-ranjan

[15] Vashisht D. Engaging and entertaining customers: Gamification in interactive marketing. In: The Palgrave Handbook of Interactive Marketing. Cham: Springer International Publishing; 2023. pp. 807-835

[16] Robson K, Plangger K, Kietzmann JH, McCarthy I, Pitt L. Game on: Engaging customers and employees through gamification. Business Horizons. 2016;**59**(1):29-36. DOI: 10.1016/j.bushor.2015.08.002

[17] Marriott Bonvoytm Rewards Program [Internet]. Marriott.com. Available from: https:// marriott.com/loyalty.mi

[18] Bardukova L. Navigating the hospitality horizon: Current trends and strategies for customer attraction and retention in the hotel industry. Economics and Computer Science. 2023;(2):88-103. Available from: https://ideas.repec.org/a/kab/journl/y2023i2p88-103.html

[19] Tuah NM, Ahmedy F, Gani A, Yong LN. A survey on gamification for health rehabilitation care: Applications, opportunities, and open challenges. Information (Basel). 2021;**12**(2):91. DOI: 10.3390/info12020091

[20] Sik-Lanyi C, Szucs V, Shirmohammadi S, Grudeva P, Abersek B, Guzsvinecz T, et al. How to develop serious games for social and cognitive competence of children with learning difficulties. Acta Polytechnica Hungarica. 2019;**16**(5):149-169. DOI: 10.12700/aph.16.6.2019.6.10

[21] WM IJ, van Goor H, Rosman C, Luursema JM. The fun factor: Does serious gaming affect the volume of voluntary laparoscopic skills training? World Journal of Surgery. 2021;**45**(1):66-71. DOI: 10.1007/s00268-020-05800-y

[22] Rivera JMS, Piñate EEN. Video game based on the game-based learning methodology as a means of communication for the formation of eating habits in children with celiac disease. Revista de Comunicación de la SEECI. 2021;(53):83-100

[23] H-Man [Internet]. Articares. Available from: https://articares.com/h-man/

[24] Szücs V, Guzsvinecz T, Magyar A. Movement pattern recognition in physical rehabilitation—Cognitive motivation-based IT method and algorithms. Acta Polytechnica Hungarica. 2020;**17**(2):211-235. DOI: 10.12700/aph.17.2.2020.2.12

[25] Guzsvinecz T, Szucs V, Magyar A. The cognitive motivation-based APBMR algorithm in physical rehabilitation. Acta Polytechnica Hungarica. 2023;**20**(5):41-60. DOI: 10.12700/aph.20.5.2023.5.4

[26] Donthu N, Kumar S, Pattnaik D, Lim WM. A bibliometric retrospection of marketing from the lens of psychology: Insights from Psychology & Marketing. Psychology and Marketing. 2021;**38**(5):834-865. DOI: 10.1002/mar.21472

[27] Khan MA, Pattnaik D, Ashraf R, Ali I, Kumar S, Donthu N. Value of special issues in the journal of business research: A bibliometric analysis. Journal of Business Research. 2021;**125**:295-313. DOI: 10.1016/j.jbusres.2020.12.015

[28] Cooper ID. Bibliometrics basics. Journal of the Medical Library Association. 2015;**103**(4):217-218. DOI: 10.3163/1536-5050.103.4.013

[29] Donthu N, Kumar S, Pandey N, Lim WM. Research constituents, intellectual structure, and collaboration patterns in journal of International Marketing: An Analytical Retrospective. Journal of International Marketing. 2021;**29**(2):1-25. DOI: 10.1177/1069031x211004234

[30] Verma S, Gustafsson A. Investigating the emerging COVID-19 research trends in the field of business and management: A bibliometric analysis approach. Journal of Business Research. 2020;**118**:253-261. DOI: 10.1016/j.jbusres.2020.06.057

[31] Brown T, Park A, Pitt L. A 60-year bibliographic review of the journal of advertising research: Perspectives on trends in authorship, influences, and research impact. Journal of Advertising Research. 2020;**60**(4):353-360. DOI: 10.2501/jar-2020-028

[32] Aria M, Cuccurullo C. Bibliometrix: An R-tool for comprehensive science mapping analysis. Journal of Informetrics. 2017;**11**(4):959-975. DOI: 10.1016/j.joi.2017.08.007

[33] Rodríguez-Soler R, Uribe-Toril J, De Pablo Valenciano J. Worldwide trends in the scientific production on rural depopulation, a bibliometric analysis using bibliometrix R-tool. Land Use Policy. 2020;**97**:104787. DOI: 10.1016/j.landusepol.2020.104787

[34] Radha L, Arumugam J. The research output of bibliometrics using bibliometrix R package and VOS viewer. Shanlax International Journal of Arts, Science and Humanities. 2021;**9**(2):44-49. DOI: 10.34293/sijash.v9i2.4197

[35] Zhao J, Li M. Worldwide trends in prediabetes from 1985 to 2022: A bibliometric analysis using bibliometrix R-tool. Frontiers in Public Health. 2023;**11**:1072521. DOI: 10.3389/fpubh.2023.1072521

[36] Jalal SK. Co-authorship and co-occurrences analysis using Bibliometrix R-package: A casestudy of India and Bangladesh. Annals of Library and Information Studies (ALIS). 2019;**66**(2):57-64

[37] Rodríguez MS, Ortega Alvarez AM, Vasquez L. Worldwide trends in the scientific production on soccer players market value, a bibliometric analysis using bibliometrix R-tool. Team Performance Management. An International Journal. 2022;**28**(5/6):415-440

[38] Diksha D, Chakravarty R. Global trends in the research output on sustainable development goals: A bibliometric analysis using bibliometrix R-tool. In: Futuristic Trends for Sustainable Development and Sustainable Ecosystems. Cham, Switzerland: Springer; 2022. pp. 27-47

[39] Derviş H. Bibliometric analysis using bibliometrix an R package. Journal of Scientific Research. 2020;**8**(3):156-160. DOI: 10.5530/jscires.8.3.32

[40] Omotehinwa TO. Examining the developments in scheduling algorithms research: A bibliometric approach. Heliyon. 2022;**8**(5):e09510. DOI: 10.1016/j.heliyon.2022.e09510

Chapter 2

# Gamification in Real-World Applications: Interactive Maps and Augmented Reality

*Alexandru Predescu and Mariana Mocanu*


## Abstract

This chapter delves into the dynamic realm of gamification applied to real-world scenarios, with a specific focus on the integration of geographic information systems (GIS) and augmented reality (AR). By examining case studies and current research, the potential of combining game design principles with interactive technologies is shown to create immersive and interactive experiences that enhance user engagement in complex problems across various domains such as education, health, and smart government. The large-scale adoption of interactive technologies underscores the importance of ethical considerations, inclusivity, and the potential for these technologies to foster a more connected and informed society. The chapter aims to inspire further research and practical applications in the field, focusing on the transformative power of combining gamification with GIS and AR in real-world settings.


**Keywords:** gamification, augmented reality, geographic information systems, serious games, interactive technologies

## 1. Introduction

Gamification, the art of applying game design elements and principles in non-gaming contexts, has gained significant traction across various domains, extending far beyond its origins in entertainment. This introductory section aims to establish a foundational understanding of gamification, emphasizing its core mechanics, principles, and its widespread applicability in diverse fields.

To understand the role of gamification in real-world applications, it is important to understand the significant potential that has been accumulated by the video game industry that extends beyond entertainment purposes. Over the past few decades, video games have provided dynamic cultural landscapes that foster active engagement and a sense of collaboration [1–3].

Mobile gaming represents a more recent outlet for video games, emphasizing the game design elements over hyper-realistic gameplay. From this perspective, gamification involves the translation of the engaging elements found in games, such as points, levels, challenges, and rewards, into non-game environments. This concept is not just about making activities game-like; it's about enhancing real-world interactions and experiences to be more engaging, motivating, and enjoyable. Gamification is described as the use of game design elements in non-game contexts, and fundamental research in this field offers a framework to understand its key components and implications [4].

Mobile games have played a pioneering role in real-world experiments, with activities such as treasure hunting, geocaching, urban adventure games, and massively multiplayer mobile games, representing a blend of virtual and real-world experiences. Therefore, mobile technologies combined with gamification expand the level of interaction with the digital world, improving the overall user experience over a wide range of applications.

The main challenge is finding out how gaming can provide the spark for increasing participation in the context of a given real-world application. Gamification employs a variety of mechanics to achieve its goals. These include points systems, leaderboards, achievement badges, challenges, and progress tracking. The effectiveness of these mechanics lies in their ability to tap into human psychological needs and motivations, such as the desire for achievement, competition, and social interaction [5].

Gamification has found applications in diverse fields, including education, healthcare, marketing, environmental conservation, and workplace productivity. In each of these areas, gamification serves to engage users, motivate desired behaviors, and enhance the overall experience. Real-world examples of successful gamification demonstrate the versatility and effectiveness of gamification in achieving various objectives across different sectors. In the business sector, gamification has been used to increase customer engagement and loyalty [6]. In health and wellness, gamified apps encourage users to adopt healthier habits [7]. Educational platforms use game elements to enhance student engagement and learning outcomes [8].

As gamification continues to evolve, its application is expanding into new areas, including integration with emerging technologies like augmented reality and interactive maps. The potential for gamification to revolutionize user engagement and experience in these areas is substantial, offering exciting prospects for future development [4].

Nowadays, when digital entertainment and virtual interactions have become integrated into a wide variety of applications, we find ourselves at the nexus of innovation, armed with an arsenal of tools, frameworks, and cutting-edge technologies that empower the design and implementation of diverse scenarios in practical applications [5].

The next frontier in terms of user interaction points towards encompassing interactive environments in real-world scenarios, a domain which extends across the vast landscapes of the metaverse, augmented reality (AR), and virtual reality (VR). The trend of innovation is steering towards a holistic blend of digital and physical realms, where users seamlessly navigate and engage with immersive, layered environments.

While technological advancements provide the tools and infrastructure for the realization of gamified experiences, effective game design should be based on a solid theoretical background for integrating gamification in real-world scenarios. In this sense, gamification requires a deep understanding of user motivations, preferences, and the socio-cultural landscape that define the interaction with gamified elements [9]. User-centric design principles become paramount in creating engaging experiences that resonate with diverse audiences.

This evolution signifies a paradigm shift in how we perceive and interact with our surroundings, transcending conventional boundaries into a new era of interconnected, multisensory experiences. In this dynamic landscape, the convergence of the metaverse, AR, and VR opens unprecedented avenues for creativity, collaboration, and engagement, in the context of real-world applications.

The literature review conducted for this chapter employed a comprehensive and systematic approach to identify, analyze, and synthesize relevant research on the application of gamification within real-world contexts, particularly focusing on its integration with Geographic Information Systems (GIS) and Augmented Reality (AR). The research focused preponderantly on articles published in the last 10 years, on the application of gamification and AR in real-world settings and demonstrating relevant insights into user engagement and interaction. Multiple scientific and academic databases were queried to ensure a wide coverage of the subject, including IEEE Xplore, for technical and engineering aspects of gamification, AR, and GIS technologies, and Google Scholar, for a broad spectrum of scholarly articles covering various applications and theoretical aspects of gamification. The search strategy was formulated using a combination of keywords and phrases to emphasize the interdisciplinary nature of this research: Gamification and Real-World Applications, Augmented Reality and User Engagement, Geographic Information Systems and Interactive Technologies, Game Design Principles and Educational Tools.

## 2. The synergy of gamification, interactive maps, and augmented reality

Interactive maps and AR technologies are grounded in geospatial science principles - integrating spatial data and GIS to create interactive and immersive maps [10]. These technologies are further enhanced by applying User-Centered Design (UCD) principles, ensuring that the applications are intuitive and meet user needs [11]. GIS systems, especially when combined with gamification and AR, can have a significant impact on various industries. They are instrumental in disaster management and response, transportation planning, resource management, and marketing. The ability to visualize complex data in an intuitive way makes GIS an indispensable tool in modern research and industrial applications [12].

The integration of gamification with interactive maps and AR represents a pioneering approach in various real-world applications. This section delves into how the synergy of these technologies enhances user engagement, motivation, and active involvement, thereby transforming experiences in diverse settings.

Crafting interactive experiences in digital entertainment, especially in game development, demands more than just technical expertise. In the context of mobile applications, gamification emerges as a strategy to enhance user experience, seamlessly blending user-friendly interfaces with captivating game design elements to create a distinctive package for real-world applications [4].

AR technology offers diverse integration possibilities across mobile devices, wearable tech (e.g., smartwatches, AR glasses), and various software platforms. These integrations span from visualizing 3D objects (for instance, through platforms like Augment - 3D) to enhancing navigation and tracking (for instance, in Google Maps with Live View). From an educational standpoint, AR facilitates a range of applications including real-time translation (such as Google Translate offering instant camera translation), enhancing artistic skills (as seen with SketchAR), creating engaging presentations (using tools like Aurasma for animated boards), aiding in navigation (with applications such as Spyglass offering AR-based compass and star tracker features), and augmenting photos and artworks (illustrated by LifePrint Photos and Smartify for interactive art information) [13].

Integrating GIS and AR provides a synergy to enhance user experience by overlaying detailed geospatial information onto the physical world. An in-depth investigation into the advantages of integrating GIS and AR highlights how this combination can address user experience (UX) challenges in systems employing only one of these technologies [14]. Interactive maps and AR bring a new dimension to user interaction; Maps are no longer static representations of geography but dynamic tools that can guide, educate, and entertain, while AR technology enhances GIS by overlaying digital information on the physical world, offering a more immersive way to interact with geospatial data [15].

The technical advancements and applications facilitated by this combination provide a foundation for future research in utilizing both technologies simultaneously. Significant research efforts have been directed towards the development of large scale mixed reality platforms based on real-world maps, of which GeoGuild seeks to transform mobile games into immersive social experiences [16], while VWorld and Unity have been explored for defining a universal framework for location-based game engines [17]. The challenge is to define a unified framework for the next generation of mobile games, seamlessly incorporating real-world elements with virtual environments.

This ongoing pursuit and the wider adoption of cutting-edge technologies involves tapping into existing tools and methods accessible to mobile developers. There are multiple frameworks that can be adapted to real-world applications, such as Unity, a popular development platform for its versatile capabilities and visual feedback [18, 19]. The integration of high-quality geographic data from the Google Maps database adds a dynamic layer to the gaming experience, with game objects adapting dynamically based on the user's current location [18].

Together, these studies contribute to a higher-level understanding of how gamification, coupled with advanced technologies, can redefine user engagement in the realm of mobile applications with a real-world component.

## 3. Applications in education

Society is constantly changing, while technological advancements are leaving their mark on education, moving from the traditional blackboard to digital interfaces and smart devices, with a focus on applied learning methods.

This section explores the application of gamification, interactive maps, and AR in education. Through case studies and theoretical frameworks, it illustrates how these technologies can revolutionize learning experiences, making education more immersive, enjoyable, and effective.

Gamification in education leverages game mechanics to increase student engagement and motivation. When combined with AR, it creates immersive learning experiences that are both informative and engaging. A systematic mapping study on gamification in education, demonstrates its wide-ranging applications and effectiveness in enhancing learning outcomes [20].

The integration of cutting-edge technologies in education requires an in-depth understanding of human-computer interactions [21], particularly tailored to the learning environment. Emerging technologies poised for significant impact in education encompass virtual reality (VR), augmented reality (AR), mobile learning devices, and Internet of Things (IoT) devices.

In the modern landscape, most smart devices are equipped with a GPS (Global Positioning System) component, supplying location data for diverse mobile applications, motion sensors for monitoring movements and biometric sensors. An illustrative application of smart devices in educational settings involves substituting traditional mouse and keyboard interactions with body movements or gestures, enabling the creation of mixed reality environments.

Notwithstanding the technical capabilities, the effective integration within the educational frameworks involves conducting extensive large-scale experimental evaluations to explore opportunities, address challenges, generate ideas, develop, and test solutions, define scenarios, deliver, and implement innovations, foster growth, and scalability, and ultimately instigate systemic changes.

In educational settings, combining gamification with interactive maps and AR can revolutionize the learning experience. For instance, in geography and history education, interactive maps with gamified elements can turn a conventional lesson into an engaging exploration. Similarly, AR can bring historical events to life, allowing students to experience history, and transform classroom environments by overlaying digital information onto the physical world. AR can bring complex concepts to life, offering students a more hands-on and experiential learning.

Recent studies emphasize the transformative impact of gamification in educational environments, particularly when combined with advanced technologies like AR – lessons can be gamified to include quests, challenges, and rewards, making the learning process more interactive and enjoyable [22, 23]. The tailored use of gamification in education, highlights its adaptability and capacity to cater to diverse learning styles and needs [22], while the potential of AR and gamification in education suggests that these technologies can significantly improve learning outcomes and student engagement [24].

Therefore, AR-based methodologies are gaining prominence in the vocabulary of educators, marking a paradigm shift in education by introducing innovative perspectives that bridge the educational domain with the technology-driven world. These applications range from displaying multimedia materials within the real environment to stimulating interactive learning, fostering collaboration, and enhancing immersion, underscoring the vast potential benefits of AR in educational technology [25].

Moving beyond the classroom environment, crowdsensing has emerged as one of the most prominent paradigms for harnessing the combined sensing capabilities of smartphones while raising awareness about large-scale problems with a focus on sustainability [26, 27]. The effective application of this concept for the educational domain was demonstrated in the context of an AR-based geolocation app for outdoor exploration. The EduPARK app is based on a treasure hunt format, offering a set of locations and questions to be answered by the participants to get points, with hints and feedback from a virtual mascot, providing a good example of situated learning [28].

The emerging trend of providing location-based experiences has been at the forefront of LEPLACE GLOBAL's efforts to develop an outdoor exploration platform which enables the design of interactive, geolocation-based stories with AR and gamification elements such as challenges and leaderboards [29]. The Leplace World mobile app offers immersive, self-guided tours with challenges and multimedia content. It supports various activities, including treasure hunts and educational games, tailored by means of a web platform for content designers. This facilitates educational scenarios where tour guides and teachers can create and manage interactive stories, enhancing learning through location-based activities and AR for an engaging experience, as illustrated in **Figure 1** [30].

**Figure 1.**
*AR-based geolocation app concept in educational context.*

While the benefits are significant, challenges such as technological accessibility, cost, and the need for specialized training for educators must be addressed. Furthermore, there is a growing need for empirical research to define effective implementation guidelines and to evaluate the long-term impacts of these technologies on learning outcomes and student engagement [23].

## 4. Research and applications

Gamification extends to research domains and other non-traditional gaming environments. This section showcases how gamification, interactive maps, and AR can be leveraged to increase participant involvement in real-world scenarios, enhance customer experiences, and drive innovation within various industries. Beyond education, the synergy of gamification, interactive maps, and AR finds application in various commercial and industrial domains.

In previous research, the authors conclude on the evolution of gaming towards mobile platforms, observing gaming trends and consumer preferences [3, 31]. Transitioning to mobile gaming not only reflects technological advancements but also a significant change in the gaming landscape, with mobile platforms representing a significant market segment with multiple implications for practical applications [18, 31].

In commercial settings, gamified AR apps can guide customers through a store with interactive maps, offering rewards for finding and purchasing specific items, demonstrating significant potential for increasing customer engagement and loyalty [6]. In tourism, interactive AR maps can gamify exploration, encouraging tourists to visit more locations [32]. In health and wellness, gamified apps encourage healthier habits, while in the industrial sector, gamification can be used to improve employee training, enhance productivity, and promote safety practices.

The large-scale adoption of these technologies is already recognized to enhance marketing strategies and improve measurable outcomes, offering interactive experiences that can significantly boost visitor engagement and learning. For instance, AR can overlay historical information or virtual guides over real-world locations, making tours more immersive and informative. GIS allows for personalizing recommendations based on geographical data, while gamification elements encourage exploration and interaction through rewards or challenges that can be precisely measured for effectiveness from real-time feedback [33].

In terms of research domains, crowdsensing was identified as a significant domain of convergence between game design and location-based scenarios, focusing on increasing the contribution of participants in large-scale applications. To understand the versatility and harness the potential of gamification across multiple domains of research and commercial applications, the fundamental concepts should ideally be considered as part of a high-level conceptual framework. The analysis and design of advanced gamification scenarios involve conceptual models based on Activity Theory to understand human behavior in social and organizational contexts [34]. In this sense, Clark's work in [35] introduced the concept of Serious Games (SG), characterized by their significant implications for various sectors such as e-Health, e-Commerce, and e-Learning, employing gamification to enhance user interaction and motivation.

In research settings, gamification techniques can be employed to increase participant involvement and data collection quality. For instance, gamified mobile apps can be used in environmental research to encourage data collection by citizens [36]. Solutions based on crowdsensing can prove to be essential for smart cities, allowing for monitoring areas that are not covered by fixed infrastructure while providing a direct channel of interaction between citizens and authorities [37].

There are several challenges and opportunities in designing effective crowdsensing solutions based on emerging technologies. As these technologies continue to evolve, new applications emerge across various industries. However, challenges such as balancing gamification elements to avoid over-stimulation, ensuring data privacy, and maintaining user interest over time need to be addressed.

The serious gaming approach defined in [31] outlines a georeferenced game design using dispatch optimization and reward incentives for crowdsensing tasks. The effectiveness of this approach is validated through simulations, focusing on task allocation and incentive mechanisms based on the VRP (Vehicle Routing Problem) and the VCG (Vickrey–Clarke–Groves) auction model. These models evaluate the system's performance, emphasizing the balance between participation incentives and the importance of truthful reporting for system utility.

The underlying SG platform is based on the Leplace World mobile platform designed by LEPLACE GLOBAL and the authors for citizen reporting based on crowdsensing, which uses gamification to boost engagement and interaction. The mobile app displays a map with the location of reported issues alongside player locations, featuring a responsive and visually appealing interface. The format can be adapted for specific crowdsensing scenarios, such as monitoring user-reported events in water distribution systems, as shown in **Figure 2**. The mobile application was developed in the context of the Watergame project at Politehnica University of Bucharest, demonstrating the perspectives of modern technologies in crowdsensing scenarios.

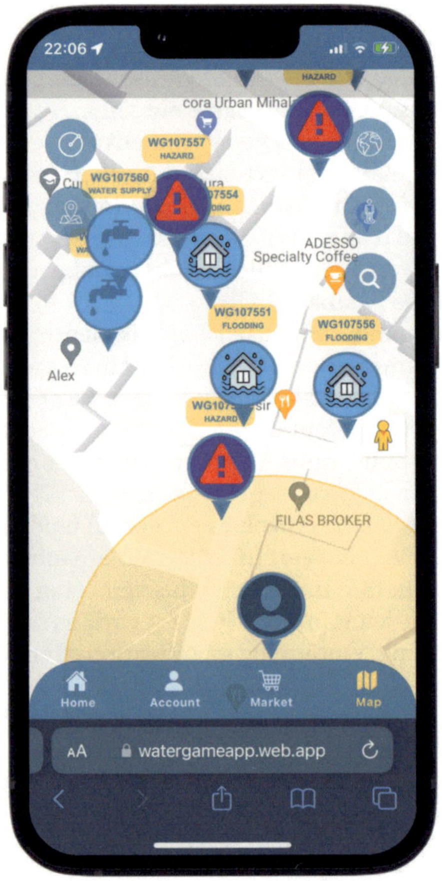


**Figure 2.**
*Watergame application.*

Considering the significance of the participants' involvement in a large-scale crowdsensing scenario, another perspective is outlined by the ParticipAct project, demonstrating how task co-creation and gamification can greatly increase user engagement. An interesting study showcases a gamification strategy to enhance sensing coverage, proving more effective than traditional incentives [38]. The research aims to boost Mobile Crowdsensing Systems (MCS) coverage for infrastructure monitoring through gamification, focusing on place-centric data collection and evaluating the overall effectiveness in a simulated environment.

A critical appraisal of the studies reviewed reveals several common limitations in the context of real-world applications. These may include, but are not limited to, small sample sizes, short-term study durations, and the reliance on self-reported data. Large-scale deployment of gamification strategies, especially those integrating GIS and AR technologies, demands significant investment in hardware, software development, and ongoing maintenance. Nonetheless, the results from simulation and real-world scenarios combined provide actionable insights.

Future research should focus on optimizing the integration of these technologies in various domains and evaluating their long-term impact. The theoretical models and practical considerations should synergize to provide new perspectives in terms of potential applications in research and commercial settings.

## 5. Practical considerations

To provide actionable insights, this section concludes with practical strategies and implementation guidelines. It provides educators, researchers, scientists, and professionals with the insights to harness the power of gamification, interactive maps, and AR in their respective fields. By exploring the intersection of gamification, interactive maps, and augmented reality, this section contributes by shedding light on innovative strategies that propel research and innovation across diverse scientific domains.

While the integration of these technologies offers numerous benefits, it also presents new challenges. Technical limitations, accessibility, and digital fragmentation are concerns that need addressing. Furthermore, there is a need for more empirical research to understand the long-term impacts of this technological synergy on various demographic groups, starting with the educational context [39].

From a technical perspective, gamification in real-world scenarios requires careful consideration of the real environment and the interactions with the physical world to be effective. In the context of MCS solutions including a broad range of technologies, there are significant technical challenges and limitations with regards to system architecture, integrations, and scalability.

The practical implications of research work in this field revolve around creating a universal platform for serious gaming across various industries, leveraging advanced AR technologies and the widespread availability of mobile devices. The primary research challenge lies in enhancing interactive sensing capabilities in MCS through AR integration. There is ongoing research focused on optimizing 3D registration and tracking of virtual objects, referencing real-world features and the need for advanced calibration methods to accurately align real and virtual worlds in a seamless blend.

The proposed solution described in related research [36, 40] emphasizes gamification and user experience on a crowdsensing platform designed to foster collaboration and participation within smart city initiatives. It also highlights potential obstacles in deploying Geospatial AR, such as correcting deviations and addressing discontinuities in gyroscope readings, underscoring the complexity of integrating AR in practical settings [40]. The results have been validated in the context of the real-life exploration game developed by LEPLACE GLOBAL, which provides an alternative representation for the interactive map, based on Geospatial AR, as shown in **Figure 3** [29].

Going forward, the integration of gamification strategies into real-world applications, especially in interactive maps and AR, is enhanced by recent technological advancements. AR/VR headsets, such as the Apple Vision Pro, have set forth the new era for AR and spatial computing, characterized by a revolutionary interaction system that leverages a three-dimensional interface, offering a natural and intuitive user experience that blends virtual and real environments – XR (eXtended Reality) [24]. The spatial operating system, enables a new paradigm allowing users to interact with digital content as if it were physically present, offering limitless possibilities for connectivity, productivity, and entertainment in gamified applications [41].

In the realm of practical applications, the innovative GIS and AR integration (XR-GIS) can be designed to map underground utilities, demonstrating the system's

**Figure 3.**
*ARMAX: Integrating AR in a location-based mobile application.*

effectiveness in real-time data collection, visualization, and communication among construction stakeholders [42]. The XR-GIS platform showcases the practical application of these technologies in improving operational efficiency and safety in construction by allowing for electronic data collection and communication on-site, stored and processed in cloud-based storage for immediate real-time decision-making.

The convergence of GIS with IoT outlines the perspectives in smart cities, enhancing urban planning, utility management, and environmental monitoring. The GIS capabilities in handling geospatial data, combined with IoT real-time data collection and monitoring, can foster the development of integrated systems allowing for the technical sophistication required for the seamless operation of smart infrastructure [43].

There are certain aspects regarding the practical considerations that need to be addressed to enable effective gamification in the realm of GIS and AR-based applications, considering the implementation guidelines, and domains of application, as outlined in **Table 1**.

The practical considerations of incorporating gamification in real-world applications based on interactive maps and AR are significantly influenced by a spectrum of technologies beyond the smartphone. The combined features of these devices not only redefine user engagement but also ensure social connectivity, immersive experiences, and data security. As the field of spatial computing evolves, the synergy between these technologies will continue to shape the future of gamification in real-world applications.

| Practical considerations | Guidelines | Domains | References |
|---|---|---|---|
| Integration and Compatibility | Utilize open standards and APIs, test across platforms, employ middleware solutions | All domains using these technologies | [42, 44, 45] |
| UI/UX design | Design intuitive UIs, focus on minimizing latency (AR), user-centered design, usability testing | Education, AR applications, gamified platforms | [14, 20, 46] |
| Scalability and Performance | Use cloud services, optimize data algorithms, scalable system design | High-traffic applications, AR in large-scale environments | [47–49] |
| Data Accuracy and Reliability | Use reliable data sources, ensure regular updates, validation checks | GIS applications, AR-based navigation and exploration | [31, 50] |
| Accessibility and Inclusivity | Adhere to accessibility standards, inclusive design, features for diverse user groups | Educational tools, public-facing applications | [51–53] |
| Privacy and Security | Robust security measures, compliance with privacy laws, transparency in data usage | All domains, especially those handling personal and location data | [54, 55] |
| Technological Limitations and User Adoption | Design with current tech limitations in mind, provide training and support | Fields new to AR, gamification, and interactive maps | [56] |
| Evaluating Effectiveness and ROI | Develop specific metrics, track engagement and usage, assess improvements | Corporate training, educational applications, marketing strategies | [57, 58] |

**Table 1.**
*Practical considerations.*

## 6. Conclusions

In this chapter, we have explored the transformative potential of integrating GIS and AR within the realm of gamification, highlighting its significant impact on user experience across various real-world applications. The convergence of these technologies has been shown not only to enhance user engagement and interaction but also to provide innovative solutions to complex problems in education, health, urban planning, and beyond. The examples provided underscore the versatility and adaptability of gamification, interactive maps, and AR, illustrating their capability to create immersive, engaging experiences that transcend traditional boundaries.

As we look towards the future, the synergy between GIS, AR, and gamification will continue to evolve, driven by technological advancements and a deeper understanding of user engagement dynamics. While the potential for these technologies to revolutionize learning, improve health outcomes, and foster community engagement is vast, it requires continued research, thoughtful implementation, and a commitment to user-centric design principles. Embracing these challenges and opportunities brings about a new era in digital interaction, where the boundaries between the physical and virtual worlds become increasingly blurred, offering unprecedented possibilities for innovation and impact in real-world applications.

Acknowledging the work of pioneers in the field and the ongoing efforts of researchers and practitioners, this chapter aims to inspire further exploration and development within the gamification community. As we advance, it is essential to maintain a focus on ethical considerations, accessibility, and inclusivity, ensuring that the benefits of GIS, AR, and gamification are effectively represented. With a collaborative approach and a commitment to excellence, the future of gamification in real-world applications promises a more engaged, informed, and connected world.

## Acknowledgements

The examples provided are based on the work of LEPLACE GLOBAL, a tech startup in the industry of augmented reality and location-based mobile games, co-founded by the first author of this chapter.

## Conflict of interest

The authors declare no conflict of interest.

## Author details

Alexandru Predescu* and Mariana Mocanu
National University of Science and Technology Politehnica Bucharest, Bucharest, Romania

*Address all correspondence to: alexandru.predescu@upb.ro

## References

[1] Shliakhovchuk E, Muñoz GA. Intercultural perspective on impact of video games on players: Insights from a systematic review of recent literature. Educational Sciences: Theory and Practice. 2020;**20**(1):40-58

[2] Garcia-Fernandez J, Medeiros L. Cultural heritage and communication through simulation videogames—A validation of minecraft. Heritage. 2019;**2**(3):2262-2274

[3] Predescu A, Mocanu M. A data driven survey of video games. In: In: 2020 12th International Conference on Electronics, Computers and Artificial Intelligence (ECAI). Bucharest, Romania: IEEE; 2020. pp. 1-6

[4] Deterding S, Dixon D, Khaled R, Nacke L. From game design elements to Gamefulness: Defining "gamification". In: Proceedings of the 15th International Academic MindTrek Conference: Envisioning Future Media Environments [Internet]. New York, NY, USA: Association for Computing Machinery; 2011. pp. 9-15. (MindTrek'11). DOI: 10.1145/2181037.2181040

[5] Hamari J, Koivisto J, Sarsa H. Does gamification work? – A literature review of empirical studies on gamification. In: 2014 47th Hawaii International Conference on System Sciences. IEEE; 2014. pp. 3025-3034

[6] Hastuti J, Honeyta P, Chan S. Effect of gamification principles and perceived ease of use of gamification in mobile devices on customer engagement and flow state to increase mobile shopping loyalty of shopee marketplace users. International Journal of Management and Economics Invention [Internet]. 2022;**8**(10):2667-2674. DOI: 10.5281/zenodo.7199339

[7] Saprikis V, Vlachopoulou M. A Literature review and an investigation on gamified mobile apps in health and fitness. In: Matsatsinis NF, Kitsios FC, Madas MA, Kamariotou MI, editors. Operational Research in the Era of Digital Transformation and Business Analytics. BALCOR 2020. Springer Proceedings in Business and Economics. Cham: Springer; 2023. DOI: 10.1007/978-3-031-24294-6_24

[8] Paľová D, Vejačka M. Implementation of gamification principles into higher education. European Journal of Educational Research. 2022;**11**(2):763-779

[9] Rauschnabel PA, Rossmann A, tom Dieck MC. An adoption framework for mobile augmented reality games: The case of Pokémon go. Computers in Human Behavior. 2017;**76**:276-286

[10] Hruby F, Ressl R, de la Borbolla del Valle G. Linking real geographies and virtual realties with immersive geospatial technologies. In: Koutsopoulos K, de Miguel González R, Donert K, editors. Geospatial Challenges in the 21st Century [Internet]. Cham: Springer International Publishing; 2019. p. 63-79. DOI: 10.1007/978-3-030-04750-4_4

[11] Roth R, Ross K, MacEachren A. User-centered design for interactive maps: A case study in crime analysis. International Journal of Geo-Information. 2015;**4**:262-301

[12] Shrivastava R. Remote sensing and GIS in disasters management-in special reference to Asian countries. Recent Research in Science and Technology [Internet]. 2014;**6**(1): 153-156. Available from: https://updatepublishing.com/journal/index.php/rrst/article/view/1188

[13] Antonioli M, Blake C, Sparks K. Augmented reality applications in education. The Journal of Technology Studies. 2014;**40**(1/2):96-107

[14] Kim J, Lorenz M, Knopp S, Klimant P. Industrial augmented reality: Concepts and user Interface designs for augmented reality maintenance worker support systems. In: 2020 IEEE International Symposium on Mixed and Augmented Reality Adjunct (ISMAR-Adjunct). IEEE; 2020. pp. 67-69

[15] Hedley N. Augmented reality and GIS. In: Huang B, editor. Comprehensive Geographic Information Systems [Internet]. Oxford: Elsevier; 2018. pp. 355-368. Available from: https://www.sciencedirect.com/science/article/pii/B9780124095489096226

[16] Ionescu G, Valmaseda JMD, Deriaz M. GeoGuild: Location-based framework for mobile games. In: 2013 International Conference on Cloud and Green Computing. IEEE; 2013. pp. 261-265

[17] Lee A, Chang YS, Jang I. Planetary-scale geospatial open platform based on the unity3D environment. Sensors. 2020;**20**(20):5967

[18] Predescu A, Mocanu M, Chiru C. A case study of mobile games design with a real-world component based on Google maps and Unity. In: 2021 13th International Conference on Electronics, Computers and Artificial Intelligence (ECAI). IEEE; 2021. pp. 1-6

[19] Zohud T, Zein S. Cross-platform mobile app development in industry: A multiple case-study. International Journal of Computing. 2021;**20**:46-54

[20] Dicheva D, Dichev C, Agre G, Angelova G. Gamification in education: A systematic mapping study. Journal of Educational Technology & Society. 2015;**18**(3):75-88

[21] Cox MJ. Educational conflict: The problems in institutionalizing new technologies in education. In: Knowledge in the New Technologies. Frankfurt: Peter Lang Pub Inc; 2005. pp. 139-165

[22] Oliveira W, Hamari J, Shi L, Toda AM, Rodrigues L, Palomino PT, et al. Tailored gamification in education: A literature review and future agenda. Education and Information Technologies. 2023;**28**(1):373-406

[23] Zeybek N, Saygı E. Gamification in education: Why, where, when, and how?—A systematic review. Games and Culture. 2024;**19**(2):237-264

[24] Lampropoulos G, Keramopoulos E, Diamantaras K, Evangelidis G. Augmented reality and gamification in education: A systematic literature review of research, applications, and empirical studies. Applied Sciences [Internet]. 2022;**12**(13):6809. Available from: https://www.mdpi.com/2076-3417/12/13/6809

[25] Herpich F, Nunes FB, Petri G, Tarouco LMR. How mobile augmented reality is applied in education? A systematic literature review. Creative Education. 2019;**10**(07):1589

[26] Ariya, Sanjaya IM, Supangkat SH, Sembiring J. Citizen reporting through mobile crowdsensing: A smart city case of Bekasi. In: 2018 International Conference on ICT for Smart Society (ICISS). IEEE; 2018. pp. 1-4

[27] Alvear O, Calafate CT, Cano JC, Manzoni P. Crowdsensing in smart cities: Overview, platforms, and environment sensing issues. Sensors [Internet].

2018;**18**(2):460. Available from: https://www.mdpi.com/1424-8220/18/2/460

[28] Pombo L, Marques MM. The potential educational value of mobile augmented reality games: The case of EduPARK app. Education Sciences. 2020;**10**(10):287

[29] Leplace Global. Explore. Leplace [Internet]. 2023. Available from: https://www.leplace.online/ [Accessed: March 3, 2023]

[30] Predescu A, Arsene D, Mocanu M. A case study for emerging technologies and the potential applications of AR in higher education. In: 2023 24th International Conference on Control Systems and Computer Science (CSCS). IEEE; 2023. pp. 619-624

[31] Predescu A, Arsene D, Pahonțu B, Mocanu M, Chiru C. A serious gaming approach for crowdsensing in urban water infrastructure with blockchain support. Applied Sciences [Internet]. 2021;**11**(4):1449. Available from: https://www.mdpi.com/2076-3417/11/4/1449

[32] Kleftodimos A, Evagelou A, Gkoutzios S, Matsiola M, Vrigkas M, Yannacopoulou A, et al. Creating location-based augmented reality games and immersive experiences for touristic destination marketing and education. Computers. 2023;**12**(11):227

[33] Pratisto EH, Thompson N, Potdar V. Immersive technologies for tourism: A systematic review. Inf Technol Tourism. 2022;**24**(2):181-219

[34] Carvalho M, Bellotti F, Berta R, De Gloria A, Islas Sedano C, Hauge J, et al. An activity theory-based model for serious games analysis and conceptual design. Computers & Education. 2015;**87**:166-181

[35] Abt CC. Serious Games. University Press of America; 2002. 196 p. Available from: https://archive.org/details/seriousgames0000abtc

[36] Predescu A, Mocanu M. Increasing Collaboration and Participation through Serious Gaming for Improving the Quality of Service in Urban Water Infrastructure. Vol. 373, LNBIP, Lecture Notes in Business Information Processing. Cham: Springer; 2019

[37] Guo B, Yu Z, Zhou X, Zhang D. From participatory sensing to Mobile crowd sensing. In: 2014 IEEE International Conference on Pervasive Computing and Communication Workshops (PERCOM WORKSHOPS) [Internet]. Budapest, Hungary: IEEE; 2014. pp. 593-598. Available from: https://ieeexplore.ieee.org/document/6815273

[38] Talasila M, Curtmola R, Borcea C. Crowdsensing in the wild with aliens and micropayments. IEEE Pervasive Computing. 2016;**15**(1):68-77

[39] Kučak D, Pašić Đ, Mršić L. An empirical study of long-term effects of applying gamification principles to an introductory programming courses on a university level. In: Vasant P, Weber GW, Marmolejo-Saucedo JA, Munapo E, Thomas JJ, editors. Intelligent Computing & Optimization. Cham: Springer International Publishing; 2023. pp. 469-477

[40] Predescu A, Mocanu M, Lupu C. ARMAX: A Mobile geospatial augmented reality platform for serious gaming. In: Proceedings - 2019 IEEE 15th International Conference on Intelligent Computer Communication and Processing, ICCP 2019. IEEE; 2019

[41] Suzuki R, Karim A, Xia T, Hedayati H, Marquardt N. Augmented

reality and robotics: A survey and taxonomy for AR-enhanced human-robot interaction and robotic interfaces. In: Proceedings of the 2022 CHI Conference on Human Factors in Computing Systems [Internet]. New York, NY, USA: Association for Computing Machinery; 2022. (CHI'22). DOI: 10.1145/3491102.3517719

[42] Fenais A, Ariaratnam ST, Ayer SK, Smilovsky N. Integrating geographic information systems and augmented reality for mapping underground utilities. Infrastructures. 2019;**4**(4):60

[43] Safari Bazargani J, Sadeghi-Niaraki A, Choi SM. A survey of GIS and IoT integration: Applications and architecture. Applied Sciences. 2021;**11**(21):10365

[44] Geographic Information Systems: Integrating GIS and AR for Immersive Experiences [Internet]. EDIIIE. Available from: https://www.ediiie.com/blog/geographic-information-systems-integrating-gis-ar/ [Accessed: February 18, 2024]

[45] Albrecht J. Virtual geographic information system (VGIS). In: Proceedings of the Twenty-Eighth Annual Hawaii International Conference on System Sciences [Internet]. Vol. 4. IEEE; 1995. pp. 141-150. Available from: https://ieeexplore.ieee.org/document/375735 [Accessed: February 18, 2024]

[46] Syed TA, Siddiqui MS, Abdullah HB, Jan S, Namoun A, Alzahrani A, et al. In-depth review of augmented reality: Tracking technologies, development tools, AR displays, collaborative AR, and security concerns. Sensors. 2023;**23**(1):146

[47] Abdelkhalek A, Yaghi M, Alhalabi M, Gad A, Yousaf J, Hassan T, et al. Mobile-based gamification of community exercise initiatives using location services. In: 2023 10th International Conference on Future Internet of Things and Cloud (FiCloud) [Internet]. IEEE; 2023. pp. 399-403. DOI: 10.1109/FiCloud58648.2023.00064

[48] rovin-ms. Geospatial reference architecture - Azure Orbital [Internet]. 2022. Available from: https://learn.microsoft.com/en-us/azure/orbital/geospatial-reference-architecture [Accessed: February 18, 2024]

[49] Aji A, Wang F, Vo H, Lee R, Liu Q, Zhang X, et al. Hadoop GIS: A high performance spatial data warehousing system over mapreduce. Proceedings of the VLDB Endowment. 2013;**6**(11):1009-1020

[50] Hernandez-Aguilera J, Mauerman M, Osgood D. Playing to adapt: Crowdsourcing historical climate data with gamification to improve farmer's risk management instruments. SSRN Electronic Journal. 2020:1-27

[51] Ding L, Kim C, Orey M. Studies of student engagement in gamified online discussions. Computers & Education. 2017;**115**:126-142

[52] Jansen R, Mendoza FR, Hurst W. Augmented reality for supporting geo-spatial planning: An open access review. Visual Informatics. 2023;**7**(4):1-12

[53] Caselli B, Pedilarco G, Pellicelli G, Rossetti S, Zazzi M. Enhancing public space accessibility and inclusivity in residential neighbourhoods: A methodological framework and pilot application. Sustainability. 2024;**16**(4):1435

[54] Ruggiu D, Blok V, Coenen C, Kalloniatis C, Kitsiou A, Mavroeidi AG, et al. Responsible innovation at work: Gamification, public engagement, and

privacy by design. Journal of Responsible Innovation. 2022;**9**(3):315-343

[55] Aryan A, Singh S. Protecting location privacy in augmented reality using k-anonymization and pseudo-id. In: 2010 International Conference on Computer and Communication Technology (ICCCT) [Internet]. IEEE; 2010. pp. 119-124. Available from: https://ieeexplore.ieee.org/abstract/document/5640424 [Accessed: February 18, 2024]

[56] Van Krevelen R, Poelman R. A survey of augmented reality technologies, applications and limitations. International Journal of Virtual Reality. 2010;**9**:1, ISSN 1081-1451

[57] Demirci A. Evaluating the Implementation and Effectiveness of GIS-Based Application in Secondary School Geography Lessons. American Journal of Applied Sciences. 2008;**5**(3):169-178. DOI: 10.3844/ajassp.2008.169.178. Available from: https://thescipub.com/abstract/ajassp.2008.169.178

[58] Lin PJ, Kao CC, Lam KH, Tsai IC. Design and implementation of a tourism system using mobile augmented reality and GIS technologies. In: Juang J, Chen CY, Yang CF, editors. Proceedings of the 2nd International Conference on Intelligent Technologies and Engineering Systems (ICITES2013). Cham: Springer International Publishing; 2014. pp. 1093-1099. (Lecture Notes in Electrical Engineering)

Chapter 3

# Exploring Gamification in Luxury Tourism

*Ricardo Marcão, Vasco Santos and Marta Sampaio*


## Abstract

This chapter delves into the intriguing intersection of luxury tourism and gamification, examining how the incorporation of game elements and mechanics can transform the landscape of high-end travel experiences. It provides a comprehensive overview of both gamification fundamentals and the nuances of luxury tourism, highlighting their convergence and symbiotic relationship. Through a thorough exploration of successful case studies, this chapter showcases how gamification strategies can be harnessed to elevate the luxury tourism industry. We delve into the motivations driving the adoption of gamification in luxury tourism and explore innovative strategies for seamlessly integrating game-like elements into high-end travel experiences. Moreover, this chapter critically addresses the ethical considerations and challenges associated with gamification in this context, emphasizing the importance of responsible implementation. As luxury travelers increasingly seek personalized, immersive, and memorable experiences, this chapter illuminates how gamification can cater to their desires. By enhancing interactivity, personalization, and customer loyalty, gamified luxury tourism experiences are poised to shape the future of the industry. This exploration concludes with insights into emerging trends and the limitless potential that gamification holds for the ever-evolving world of luxury tourism.


**Keywords:** gamification, luxury tourism, sustainability, personalization, engagement, technology

## 1. Introduction

In an era where digital innovation seamlessly blends with consumer experiences, gamification has come to the fore as a leading strategy to captivate customers. Defined as the application of game-design principles in non-gaming scenarios, gamification has sparked interest for its potential to deeply immerse users in various sectors [1, 2]. It's in this landscape that luxury tourism, with its hallmark dedication to exceptional service and personalization, is experiencing a digital awakening. The digital-savvy luxury consumer, with refined preferences, seeks out extraordinary experiences that align with the sophistication of luxury services [3].

Luxury tourism is distinguished by its commitment to providing unparalleled experiences, superior service, and a high degree of customization. It serves a distinct market segment that values not only indulgence and luxury but also singular, unforgettable experiences [4]. As this market evolves, it seeks out fresh, innovative methods to engage and captivate its exclusive audience, with gamification emerging as a compelling approach.

Gamification's success across industries showcases its adaptability and its profound ability to enhance user engagement [5]. Its core lies in tapping into the human proclivity for play and competition, incorporating elements like point scoring and interactive challenges. In the realm of luxury tourism, gamification transcends mere amusement—it becomes an instrument to amplify the customer journey, creating an engaging narrative that enriches the exclusive offerings extended to travelers [6].

The melding of gamification with luxury tourism is rich with opportunities for ingenuity, allowing providers to design deeply resonant and emotionally engaging experiences. This fusion promises to shift the focus from service delivery to creating an experience-centric model in elite travel.

This paper scrutinizes the intricate relationship between luxury tourism and gamification, exploring the rationale behind the adoption of gamification as a strategy in this niche. It will dissect how game-like mechanisms can be intricately interwoven into the luxury travel experience, enhancing customer engagement. Through a critical examination of case studies, the paper will demonstrate gamification's capacity to innovate and retain a discerning clientele [4, 6].

Furthermore, this paper will not shy away from discussing the challenges and ethical implications of gamifying luxury tourism, advocating for a conscientious approach to ensure that such strategies meet the industry's elevated standards and expectations [5].

As luxury travelers increasingly demand not just opulence but tailored and memorable interactions, gamification emerges as a strategic avenue to satisfy these needs. By promoting interactivity, personalization, and loyalty, gamification in luxury tourism is set to leave an indelible mark on the future of this affluent industry. The ensuing sections will thus provide an extensive examination of how gamification is redefining luxury tourism and what this means for the trajectory of this sumptuous sector.

## 2. Background: emerging intersections of gamification and luxury tourism: a frontier for innovation

The confluence of gamification and luxury tourism has recently surfaced as a fertile ground for innovation and scholarly inquiry. Gamification, which entails applying game-design elements and principles in non-game contexts, possesses a distinctive set of tools for captivating and inspiring individuals. Within the realm of luxury tourism—characterized by its dedication to exclusivity, bespoke experiences, and superlative service—gamification harbors the potential to fundamentally redefine the creation and provisioning of opulent experiences. Although there is a dearth of direct research bridging these domains, there is an escalating interest in examining how gamification could amplify the quintessential elements of luxury tourism, informed by successful applications in varied industries. This article ventures into prospective research domains at the juncture of gamification and luxury tourism, underscoring personalization, exclusivity, and the insights gleanable from other market sectors.

The assimilation of gamification within luxury tourism signifies the convergence of two distinct yet progressively interrelated spheres. The scholarship on gamification is well-established, embedded in the wider discipline of behavioral science and motivational psychology, which elucidates the mechanisms by which game elements can sway consumer behavior [2]. The proliferation of digital platforms has further bolstered the embracement of gamification strategies, paving novel pathways for engendering captivating consumer engagements [5].

### 2.1 Interdisciplinary applications and strategic integration of gamification in luxury tourism

Gamification, while an interdisciplinary concept with diverse interpretations and implementations, fundamentally involves the utilization of game-design elements and principles in non-gaming contexts [1]. This encompasses the deployment of points, badges, leaderboards, and challenges aimed at engaging and motivating individuals towards goal accomplishment. The realm of gamification stretches across various domains, including education, healthcare, business, and prominently, tourism.

Within the luxury tourism sector, gamification assumes a specialized function. Scholarly perspectives articulated in Refs. [2, 5] posit that in service industries, gamification's role transcends mere entertainment, serving instead to enrich service offerings and facilitate comprehensive value creation for users. This insight gains particular pertinence in luxury tourism where the value proposition is multifaceted, transcending functional benefits to include the emotional and experiential dimensions of the consumer journey. Here, gamification emerges not as a superficial marketing tactic, but as a strategic instrument aimed at augmenting the guest experience through heightened interactivity, personalization, and memorability.

Contemporary research underscores a growing inclination towards utilizing gamification as a tool for profound and sustainable user engagement. Evidence from Ref. [2] indicates that gamification's judicious implementation can yield favorable behavioral outcomes, including escalated activity levels, enriched social interaction, and enhanced quality of user-generated content. The application of gamification, therefore, should not be perceived as a simplistic game element appendage but as an intricate part of service design, integral to cultivating a substantive rapport with the brand.

It is imperative, as per the academic discourse, to delineate gamification from akin concepts such as serious games and playful design [7]. Serious games constitute fully-developed games with explicit rules and goals, whereas gamification employs game-like mechanics in non-game environments to bolster motivation and enrich the user experience. This distinction bears significant weight in the context of luxury tourism, where gamification must be seamlessly incorporated in a manner that is congruent with the brand's ethos and the elegance of the luxury experience.

The potency of gamification is also intimately connected to its capacity to engage intrinsic motivations. Self-Determination Theory suggests that gamification can satisfy fundamental psychological needs—autonomy, competence, and relatedness—which are pivotal for fostering intrinsic motivation [8]. This consideration is especially pertinent in luxury tourism, where guests seek not just tangible rewards but experiences that align with their personal values and lifestyle aspirations.

In essence, the literature review elucidates gamification as a multifaceted construct with expansive application potential. Its successful execution in luxury tourism depends on an astute comprehension of engagement drivers and the sophisticated amalgamation of game-like elements that elevate the luxury experience.

Subsequent sections of this literature review will further elaborate on this foundation, exploring how gamification intersects with luxury tourism to enhance customer experiences, cultivate loyalty, and accrue valuable data. This exploration will also navigate the ethical considerations and pinpoint areas ripe for future scholarly inquiry.

## 2.2 Luxury tourism: catering to the quest for exclusivity and personalized experiences

Luxury tourism distinguishes itself by serving an exclusive clientele that seeks more than mere travel—these are patrons in pursuit of experiences that symbolize comfort, exclusivity, and personalization. The scholarly literature on luxury tourism posits that the quintessence of luxury lies in surpassing consumer expectations, often achieved through bespoke services that resonate with the individual's sense of identity and prestige [9]. The luxury customer experience is characterized by several key facets: impeccable service quality, an exquisite environment, and the emotional and psychological gratification derived from the experience [10].

A quintessential element of luxury tourism is the orchestration of memorable experiences. Ref. [11] contends that luxury transcends a specific set of characteristics and is instead a mindset cultivated through extraordinary and personally significant experiences. This notion is supported by research indicating a paradigm shift among luxury consumers from the acquisition of goods to the pursuit of experiences that reflect their personal ethos and ambitions [12].

The significance of personalization in augmenting the customer experience is paramount. Contemporary studies reveal that luxury travelers increasingly seek bespoke experiences tailored to their individual predilections [13]. To this end, service providers in the luxury tourism realm are employing sophisticated data analytics and customer relationship management tools to offer highly personalized services that foster a sense of exclusivity and distinctiveness [14].

Furthermore, the luxury tourism experience is intimately associated with the pursuit of authenticity. Authentic experiences are hallmarked by genuineness, cultural immersion, and a profound connection with the local milieu—elements that luxury travelers are seeking with greater vigor [15]. Authenticity also encompasses the personal transformation and enlightenment travelers often seek through their voyages, as suggested by studies on transformative travel experiences [16].

The literature also underscores the challenges confronting the luxury tourism sector in sustaining exceptional customer experiences. With customer expectations ever-escalating, the imperatives of continual innovation, and the imperative management of service excellence emerge as recurrent themes [17]. Moreover, reconciling exclusivity with inclusivity and ensuring sustainability in the offerings presented are increasingly emphasized as areas of concern [18].

In summation, the literature review on luxury tourism underscores the necessity of delivering unparalleled service, tailored personalization, authentic encounters, and indelible experiences. It implies that providers in the luxury tourism industry must persist in their innovation and adaptability to cater to the changing predilections of their clientele, all while upholding the exclusivity and lofty standards that hallmark the luxury domain.

This paper presents a structured exploration into the innovative nexus of gamification and luxury tourism, dissecting the potential of game mechanics to revolutionize the high-end travel experience. Following the introduction, Section 2 lays the foundational background, discussing the emergent intersection of gamification principles and luxury tourism's quest for exclusivity. Section 3 unpacks various theoretical frameworks, including behavioral psychology, service marketing, and information systems theories, that inform the strategic implementation of gamification. Section 4 dives into empirical case studies, offering tangible insights into the application and impact of gamification within the context of luxury tourism and beyond. The subsequent sections prognosticate the future directions of gamification in this sector, with a particular focus on emerging technologies, sustainability, personalization, social engagement, digital rewards, and the accompanying regulatory and ethical considerations. The paper concludes by synthesizing the findings, underscoring the transformative potential of gamification in enhancing customer engagement, fostering brand loyalty, and contributing to sustainable luxury tourism practices, while also pointing out areas ripe for future research.

### 2.3 Empirical insights on gamification in luxury tourism

Empirical research on gamification spans various contexts, with notable investigations into education, healthcare, business productivity, and consumer behavior. In luxury tourism, empirical findings shed light on gamification's capacity to enrich customer experiences, sway consumer behavior, and bolster service providers' value proposition.

Studies have consistently affirmed that gamification can exert a positive influence on customer experiences and behaviors. For instance, Ref. [19] revealed that gamification components such as points and leaderboards significantly boost customer engagement and duration of interaction with service platforms. Another empirical investigation detailed in Ref. [20] concluded that gamification elevates perceived enjoyment and service usage intentions. These outcomes hold particular pertinence for luxury tourism, where elevated engagement and enjoyment are integral to the customer experience paradigm.

Focusing on cultural and educational tourism—a frequent aspect of luxury travel—gamification has been leveraged to amplify educational engagement. An empirical study by Ref. [21] within museum settings found that gamified learning notably enhances the exploratory process and information retention. This insight suggests that luxury tourism environments could effectively incorporate gamification to enrich educational and cultural experiences.

Attention has also been directed towards gamification's role in cultivating consumer loyalty and retention. Research embodied in Ref. [22] indicates that gamification can heighten customer retention rates and the propensity to recommend services to others, which aligns with the strategic imperatives of luxury tourism enterprises that prioritize customer allegiance.

Furthermore, empirical analyses underscore gamification's utility in enabling data-driven personalization. As outlined in Ref. [23], gamification mechanisms serve as conduits for accumulating consumer data, facilitating the customization of services to align with individual consumer preferences. Such personalized strategies not only refine the customer experience but also amplify the efficacy of marketing endeavors.

Conversely, empirical studies caution against the pitfalls of gamification's misapplication. Ref. [24] warns that gamification, if ineffectively executed, can diminish intrinsic motivation and potentially tarnish brand reputation—outcomes that luxury tourism must diligently avoid.

Longitudinal research on gamification, although limited, yields vital perspectives on the enduring effects of gamified interventions. A longitudinal analysis presented in Ref. [25] intimates that despite gamification's initial surge in engagement, its sustained success necessitates iterative strategy refinements to meet evolving consumer expectations and behaviors.

In essence, the empirical body of work on gamification delineates a spectrum of advantages, from augmenting the luxury tourism experience and stimulating educational discovery to nurturing loyalty and enabling bespoke marketing tactics. Nevertheless, it concurrently highlights the imperative of astute gamification execution and the dynamic management of gamified initiatives to ensure congruity with brand ethos and enduring customer satisfaction.

### 2.4 Leveraging gamification for enhanced customer engagement and brand loyalty in luxury tourism

The strategic incorporation of gamification to boost customer engagement and foster brand allegiance has garnered substantial academic interest, particularly within industries where the customer experience is of paramount importance. Luxury tourism is a prime candidate for such strategies, given that the bond between guests and the brand is as critical as the lavishness of the services rendered.

Empirical research has reliably demonstrated that gamification can amplify customer engagement. Ref. [22], for instance, illustrates that gamification methods, such as challenges and reward systems, can markedly escalate user activity on digital interfaces. Within the sphere of luxury tourism, this equates to more profound brand interactions, whether through immersive virtual experiences, loyalty applications, or interactive engagements that encourage active participation and extend involvement.

Furthermore, the deployment of gamification mechanisms has been linked to heightened brand loyalty. Ref. [26] reveals that when gamified services are perceived as pleasurable and empowering, they can enhance the emotional bond with the brand, thereby intensifying loyalty. This is corroborated by Ref. [27], who notes that the bespoke recognition afforded by gamification cultivates a robust brand community, reinforcing loyalty among luxury clientele.

These studies also suggest that gamification can elevate the perceived value of a service or experience, which is indispensable in the luxury tourism industry. As indicated by Ref. [19], integrating gamification into service offerings can bolster users' value perceptions, incentivizing them to revisit and promote the service to peers. Such perceived value transcends concrete advantages, including the social and psychological incentives derived from gamified participation.

Research by Ref. [28] delves into how gamification can stimulate repeat patronage, a cornerstone of customer fidelity. Incremental rewards and the acknowledgement of customer milestones can encourage recurring business, thus boosting the customer's lifetime value to the brand. In the luxury domain, where personalized attention and exclusivity are anticipated, these tactics require delicate execution to maintain brand integrity and meet guest expectations.

Nonetheless, sustaining engagement through gamification is not without its challenges. Inappropriately aligned or complex gamification elements may deter rather than attract users, as pointed out by Ref. [29], who advocates for crafting gamification systems that resonate with users' intrinsic motivators and reflect their core values.

The synergy between technological advancements and gamification holds particular promise in luxury tourism. Innovations in mobile technology, augmented reality, and artificial intelligence pave the way for novel gamified experiences. Ref. [30] suggests these technologies can revolutionize loyalty schemes and customer interactions, providing fresh methods for engagement in luxurious environments.

In summation, gamification stands out as an influential instrument for bolstering engagement and loyalty in luxury tourism. Empirical findings advocate that, when executed with insight and sensitivity, gamification can substantially enhance a luxury brand's appeal, forging enduring emotional connections, encouraging repeat visitation, and cultivating a dedicated clientele.

### 2.5 Data and analytics: pivotal elements in gamification strategies for luxury tourism

In an era increasingly driven by digital innovation, data and analytics have become essential components in the strategic development of gamification. This is particularly true in the luxury tourism sector, where a deep understanding of customer preferences and behaviors is essential for curating personalized experiences. Scholarly literature sheds light on how data gleaned from gamified interactions can be leveraged to heighten customer engagement and reinforce brand loyalty.

Empirical research has delved into gamification's efficacy in amassing comprehensive consumer data. For example, Ref. [31] found that gamified applications could incentivize users to voluntarily disclose their preferences and actions, providing a treasure trove of insights for businesses intent on customizing their services. In the realm of luxury tourism, where services are often tailor-made, such data is pivotal in sculpting experiences that precisely mirror individual customer desires.

The literature, particularly Ref. [23], underscores gamification's capability to drive service personalization, a critical expectation among luxury travelers. Through game mechanics that monitor user decisions and accomplishments, companies can extract patterns and predilections that facilitate the fine-tuning of services, thereby elevating the luxury experience to unprecedented heights.

The enrichment of Customer Relationship Management (CRM) systems through gamification has also been recognized. Ref. [32] suggests that gamified CRM platforms can forge deeper insights into customer needs and behavioral tendencies, enabling businesses to anticipate future trends and make informed strategic choices. For luxury brands, which prioritize cultivating lasting customer connections, such insights are invaluable.

Gamification can also significantly bolster marketing strategies within the luxury tourism sector. A study by Ref. [24] indicates that the detailed metrics on customer engagement procured through gamification enable marketers to pinpoint the most impactful touchpoints and devise campaigns that resonate strongly with their intended audience.

However, with the vast potential of data and analytics in gamification comes ethical considerations, especially concerning privacy and data security. The academic discourse advocates for striking a delicate balance between collecting data to enhance customer experiences and maintaining customer privacy, a principle especially critical in luxury tourism where discretion is paramount [33].

Additionally, the sustainability of gamification initiatives can be quantified and optimized through data analytics. By evaluating long-term engagement patterns and behavioral trends, businesses can adapt their gamification strategies to ensure enduring attractiveness and relevance to luxury travelers [19].

In summation, the literature review accentuates the significance of data and analytics in the gamification landscape of luxury tourism. Strategic data utilization not only facilitates the personalization of customer experiences but also fortifies CRM systems and shapes robust marketing strategies, significantly contributing to sustained customer engagement and brand loyalty. Nevertheless, it simultaneously casts light on the necessity for ethical data management practices to preserve customer trust and uphold the luxury tourism industry's esteemed standards.

## 2.6 Ethical practices and sustainable strategies in gamification for luxury tourism

The fusion of gamification with luxury tourism brings to the forefront critical discussions on ethics and sustainability—concepts of growing significance as the industry evolves. Scholarly literature underscores the necessity for ethical gamification practices, emphasizing respect for user autonomy, stringent data privacy, and the enduring impact of gamification initiatives.

A salient ethical concern in gamification is the potential for consumer manipulation. Ref. [34] explores the delicate balance between engaging customers and inadvertently manipulating them through gamification mechanics. This issue is particularly acute in luxury tourism, where customers possess acute discernment. Ethical gamification demands transparency, explicit user consent, and congruence with the users' objectives and aspirations.

In our data-centric world, the sanctity of privacy and the assurance of security are critical. Luxury travelers often expect exceptional levels of discretion, placing the ethical management of their data at the forefront of industry priorities. Ref. [35] contends that the stewardship of customer data must be underpinned by robust privacy protocols to preserve and protect the trust inherent in the customer-brand relationship.

Sustainability in gamification extends beyond initial user engagement, aiming to foster sustained interaction and allegiance. According to Ref. [36], gamification strategies must engender lasting value, as opposed to ephemeral thrills. For the luxury tourism market, gamification should integrate seamlessly into the overarching brand story and customer journey, rather than serving as an isolated attraction.

Moreover, environmental sustainability emerges as an essential consideration in luxury tourism. The sector is tasked with devising gamification approaches that encourage eco-conscious behaviors among its clientele. For instance, gamification techniques can incentivize guests to engage in sustainable practices during their travels [37].

Cultural sensitivity and inclusivity are equally imperative. As gamified tourism experiences frequently traverse cultural boundaries, they must be crafted with a keen understanding of cultural distinctions to ensure respectfulness and inclusiveness [38].

Additionally, luxury tourism providers employing gamification must adeptly navigate a complex web of international regulations and standards, particularly in scenarios involving cross-border data exchanges. Adhering to comprehensive legal frameworks like the General Data Protection Regulation (GDPR) is vital for the ethical and lawful handling of customer data related to gamification [39].

The review of pertinent literature indicates that while gamification offers considerable promise for enriching the luxury tourism experience, it must be executed within a robust ethical structure. This structure should honor customer autonomy, safeguard data privacy, and embrace sustainability in its multifaceted forms. The sustained success of gamification in the luxury tourism industry hinges on its ability to uphold ethical integrity, encourage responsible practices, and remain committed to the overarching principles of cultural sensitivity and regulatory adherence.

## 2.7 Identifying research gaps and charting future directions in gamification within luxury tourism

Although scholarly interest in gamification as it applies to luxury tourism is expanding, significant research gaps remain, which must be addressed to fully harness gamification's potential in this domain. Future research is pivotal in guiding both scholars and industry practitioners towards the development of more sophisticated and enduring gamification strategies.

A notable void in the current literature is the long-term effects of gamification on customer behavior and brand allegiance within the luxury tourism industry. Despite studies on immediate engagement, there is a discernible need for longitudinal research that scrutinizes gamification's influence on enduring customer retention and sustained brand loyalty over extended periods [22].

The cross-cultural reception of gamification also requires comprehensive investigation. Given that luxury tourism caters to a global audience, it is imperative to understand the differential impacts of gamification across diverse cultural landscapes. Future research must delve into the cultural sensitivities that could shape the reception and efficacy of gamification strategies [40].

Furthermore, the confluence of gamification with cutting-edge technologies like VR, AR, and AI presents new avenues for augmenting the luxury tourism experience. Empirical research is warranted to evaluate how these technologies can be synergized with gamification to elevate the luxury travel narrative [41].

Another fertile area for investigation is the role of big data in personalizing gamified experiences. As luxury tourism entities amass extensive datasets, there is an emergent need to discern how this information can be harnessed to devise profoundly personalized and ethically sound gamification strategies, ensuring compliance with stringent privacy and data protection statutes [42].

The promotion of sustainable tourism practices through gamification is an area ripe for exploration. Future studies could assess how gamification can incentivize sustainable choices among luxury tourists and gauge its effectiveness in fostering environmental stewardship [43].

Ethical considerations related to gamification, particularly the risks of addiction or exploitation, necessitate further scholarly attention. Future research endeavors should strive to formulate ethical frameworks and best practices for gamification, safeguarding its positive contribution to consumer welfare [44].

Lastly, the economic implications and ROI of gamification initiatives in luxury tourism remain underexplored. Subsequent studies should endeavor to quantify the tangible benefits of gamification, thereby equipping providers with critical data to inform strategic investments in gamification endeavors [19].

Exploring these uncharted areas of research will substantially contribute to our understanding of gamification's role in luxury tourism. Such academic endeavors are expected to lead the industry towards developing luxury travel experiences that are not only engaging and tailored to individual needs but also adhere to ethical standards and prove to be economically beneficial.

## 3. Theoretical frameworks

The exploration of gamification within luxury tourism is underpinned by a multidisciplinary theoretical framework, drawing from behavioral psychology, service marketing, and information systems. The subsequent subsections delineate the principal theories foundational to the application and efficacy of gamification.

### 3.1 Behavioral psychology theories

Behavioral psychology provides the groundwork for discerning how gamification can modulate human behavior, especially within the ambit of luxury tourism. These theories elucidate the effectiveness of gamification elements such as points, badges, and leaderboards in altering behaviors, cultivating engagement, and nurturing loyalty.

Classical conditioning, introduced by Ivan Pavlov, and operant conditioning, expanded upon by B.F. Skinner, are seminal behavioral psychology concepts with direct implications for gamification. Classical conditioning fosters associations between a conditioned stimulus and a consequent response, while operant conditioning reinforces behaviors with rewards or deterrents. Within the luxury tourism domain, these principles elucidate the propensity for the expectation of rewards to engender recurring utilization of gamified services. Albert Bandura's Social Learning Theory advocates that learning is a social endeavor, occurring through observation, imitation, and modeling. This theory is pertinent to gamification, where witnessing and replicating the rewarded actions of others in a system, such as a luxury resort's loyalty program, can galvanize tourists to participate similarly [38].

Cognitive Evaluation Theory (CET), a subset of Self-Determination Theory (SDT), underscores the influence of intrinsic and extrinsic motivators on behavior. CET posits that the manner in which rewards are framed can affect one's intrinsic motivation. For instance, rewards that are perceived as controlling or that diminish an individual's autonomy can inadvertently dampen intrinsic motivation [45]. In luxury tourism, it is imperative that rewards are thoughtfully curated to bolster the guest's autonomy and competence, not merely serve as extrinsic incentives.

Csikszentmihalyi's Flow Theory, which is particularly germane to gamification, characterizes a state of profound immersion and concentrated focus, where the individual is so engrossed in an activity that external distractions fade into insignificance [46]. In the sphere of luxury tourism, gamification strategies can be devised to catalyze flow by presenting challenges that resonate with a guest's skill set, fostering profound engagement with the activity or service offered.

The Theory of Planned Behavior (TPB) posits that behavioral intentions, steered by attitudes, social norms, and perceived control, are the harbingers of action. This theory can guide the structuring of gamification components to be congruent with the values and norms of luxury tourists, thereby shaping their intent to partake in gamified endeavors [47].

The Transtheoretical Model of Behavior Change, also known as the Stages of Change Model, developed by Prochaska and DiClemente, delineates the phases individuals traverse in modifying behavior. Gamification can bolster behavior transformation by supplying stage-specific interventions, ranging from awareness enhancement to the sustenance of new behaviors [48]. For example, in luxury tourism, gamification mechanisms can navigate guests from an emergent curiosity to a lasting engagement with environmental conservation activities advocated by eco-friendly resorts.

These behavioral psychology theories furnish a robust scaffolding for interpreting and forecasting the ways in which gamification can mold the conduct of luxury tourists. By harnessing these theoretical perspectives, providers in luxury tourism can forge gamified experiences that are not only captivating and delightful but also in harmony with the psychological needs and aspirations of their clientele.

### 3.2 Service marketing theories

Service marketing theories provide a lens through which we can understand the enhancement of service marketing by gamification, especially within the luxury tourism sector. These theories highlight the distinctive attributes of services and the strategies for their effective marketing.

The Service-Dominant (S-D) Logic, as introduced by Vargo and Lusch in Refs. [49, 50], transitions the focus from traditional goods-dominant logic by underscoring the intangible facets of services and the critical importance of co-creating value between providers and consumers. In the realm of gamification, luxury tourism providers can adopt this framework to craft experiences that foster active customer participation and joint creation of the luxury experience.

The Extended Marketing Mix, or the 7 Ps (Product, Price, Place, Promotion, People, Process, Physical Evidence), takes on particular significance in service marketing due to its inclusion of service-specific elements. Gamification can be woven into each of these facets, such as through gamified advertising campaigns, improving service delivery processes with game elements, or embedding gamified interactions within the physical ambiance of a luxury hotel [51].

The GAP Model, as delineated by Parasuraman, Zeithaml, and Berry in Ref. [52], pinpoints the disparities between customer expectations and actual experiences that can influence service quality perceptions. Gamification can serve to bridge these gaps by instituting feedback mechanisms and rewards that cater to customer needs and heighten the perceived quality of service. For example, gamification features within a customer service portal could offer instant recognition and problem resolution, thus cultivating a more favorable perception of the service.

The Moments of Truth Model, put forth by Carlzon in Ref. [53], alludes to those critical interactions where customers form lasting impressions of the service. Gamification can render these moments more remarkable and positive. A luxury resort, for instance, could implement a gamified check-in process to generate an entertaining and inviting first impression that establishes the tone for the guest's entire stay.

Pine and Gilmore, in Ref. [10], conceived the concept of the experience economy, postulating that businesses should design memorable events for customers, transforming memory into a service. Gamification in luxury tourism has the capacity to forge such indelible experiences by employing interactive storytelling, challenges, and personalized adventures that immerse guests in their travel narrative.

This theoretical perspective accentuates the enduring relationships between businesses and their customers, transcending beyond mere transactions. In the domain of luxury tourism, gamification can serve as an instrument for nurturing and sustaining these relationships by stimulating continuous engagement and offering rewards for loyal patronage [54].

Service marketing theories propose a foundational framework for the integration of gamification into luxury tourism marketing strategies. They contend that gamification should be synergized as a component of a comprehensive approach aimed at enriching service quality, crafting unforgettable experiences, and cultivating long-term patron connections. By leveraging these theories in the conceptualization and execution of gamification, luxury tourism operators can devise distinct and value-enriched services that resonate with the expectations of affluent travelers.

### 3.3 Information systems theories

Information Systems (IS) theories provide a framework for understanding the role of technology in supporting and improving business processes, including marketing and customer engagement strategies like gamification. These theories elucidate the principles behind the design, implementation, and evaluation of gamified systems within the luxury tourism sector.

The Technology Acceptance Model (TAM), as introduced in Ref. [55], posits that the adoption of technology is predominantly influenced by its perceived usefulness and ease of use. In the gamification context, TAM can inform the design of gamified elements in luxury tourism services, ensuring they are user-friendly and deemed valuable by customers.

The Unified Theory of Acceptance and Use of Technology (UTAUT), building upon TAM as per Ref. [56], presents a more elaborate framework incorporating additional determinants like social influence and facilitating conditions. UTAUT provides insights into how social factors may affect guests' interactions with gamified experiences in luxury tourism environments.

Diffusion of Innovations Theory, as described in Ref. [57], offers a perspective on how new ideas, products, or technologies propagate through societies or individual cohorts. Within gamification, this theory aids luxury tourism providers in strategizing the rollout of gamified features to guarantee their acceptance and appreciation by customers.

The Information Systems Success Model provides a multi-dimensional approach to evaluate the success of information systems, including aspects like system quality, information quality, service quality, usage intentions, user satisfaction, and net benefits. This model can be applied to gauge the impact of gamified systems on improving the luxury tourism experience and achieving business goals, such as heightened customer loyalty and engagement [28].

Researchers have adapted Csikszentmihalyi's Flow Theory to the IS domain, investigating how systems can be crafted to induce an optimal user experience characterized by a deep state of immersion or flow. In luxury tourism, gamified systems that catalyze this state are likely to significantly elevate the guest experience by fostering profound engagement and satisfaction [46].

Affordance Theory in IS research, which has its roots in Gibson's original concept from 1979, concentrates on the attributes of technology that afford users the possibility to perform specific actions. Understanding the affordances of digital platforms is pivotal in creating features that stimulate user participation and interaction in the luxury tourism narrative [7].

IS theories impart crucial insights into the conceptualization, adoption, and assessment of gamified experiences in the realm of luxury tourism. By comprehending factors such as user acceptance of technology, and the social and psychological aspects that influence technology usage, luxury tourism operators can devise gamified experiences that significantly bolster customer engagement and satisfaction. The application of these theories necessitates a delicate equilibrium between technological innovation and the personalized, high-touch services that epitomize luxury tourism.

### 3.4 Sustainability theories

Sustainability theories provide a comprehensive framework for understanding the application of gamification as a means to foster sustainable practices within the luxury tourism industry. These theories underscore the significance of environmental conservation, social responsibility, and economic stability, advocating for a well-rounded approach to sustainability that can be augmented through gamified initiatives.

The Triple Bottom Line (TBL) theory, put forward by John Elkington in 1997, advocates for businesses to extend their commitment beyond profits to include social and environmental concerns—denoted as the three Ps: People, Planet, and Profit.

Within the gamification sphere, luxury tourism operators have the opportunity to cultivate experiences that incentivize guests to adopt sustainable behaviors, such as minimizing energy use or engaging in local conservation projects, thus supporting the social and environmental dimensions of the TBL [7].

Ecological Modernization Theory proposes that economic advancement and environmental conservation can be mutually reinforcing objectives. This perspective highlights the pivotal role of innovation and technology in realizing sustainable progress [7]. In this vein, gamification emerges as a strategic instrument for ecological modernization within luxury tourism, merging sustainable practices with guest experiences via novel and captivating technologies that endorse environmental guardianship.

Although The Theory of Planned Behavior (TPB) is broadly focused on behavioral insights, its relevance to sustainable conduct is noteworthy. According to TPB, individual behavior is directed by attitudes, subjective norms, and perceived control over the behavior [47]. Gamification can harness these elements to propel tourists towards sustainability by cultivating a favorable mindset, establishing a normative framework for sustainable actions, and empowering guests to recognize their capacity to effect change.

Social Cognitive Theory spotlights the mechanisms of observational learning, imitation, and modeling as instrumental in altering behavior. In the luxury tourism sector, gamified components can be employed to exhibit sustainable practices undertaken by role models or peers, thus inspiring guests to replicate these actions. This strategy is particularly potent when guests witness the accolades or benefits accorded to those who participate in sustainable endeavors [38].

The Diffusion of Innovation Theory, referenced in [57], elucidates the process through which novel and sustainable practices can gain traction and spread among consumers within luxury tourism. Gamification can act as a catalyst for innovation in sustainability, rewarding early adopters and sharing their experiences to promote broader adoption of sustainable behaviors among the tourist demographic.

Stakeholder Theory posits that businesses should account for the interests of all stakeholders, including the community and the environment, within their operational strategies [58]. Gamification strategies can be intentionally designed to resonate with the objectives of diverse stakeholders in luxury tourism, such as waste reduction for environmental benefit or supporting local communities via cultural heritage activities.

Sustainability theories lay a solid foundation for integrating gamification into luxury tourism in a manner that upholds environmental integrity, societal welfare, and economic health. Leveraging these theoretical frameworks allows luxury tourism providers to devise gamified experiences that not only elevate the guest experience but also contribute to the common good, ensuring the sector's endurance and ethical responsibility amidst global sustainability challenges.

Each theory enriches the multifaceted comprehension of gamification's role in luxury tourism, aiming to enhance client experiences, inspire positive conduct, and support the sustainable evolution of the industry.

## 4. Case studies

Exploring the application of gamification in luxury tourism and related fields reveals a range of innovative strategies aimed at enhancing visitor experiences, engaging audiences more deeply, and promoting sustainable behaviors. Let us consider the following case studies that showcase the diverse and impactful use of gamification.

### 4.1 Sustainable tourism through gamification

Ref. [59] examines gamification techniques and their application in promoting sustainable tourism activities. The paper illustrates how gamification acts as a bridge connecting tourists, organizations, and communities, fostering a responsible and ethical approach to tourism. By analyzing success stories within the hospitality and tourism industry, the study underscores the role of gamification in improving sustainable practices by engaging tourists, employees, and local communities in the economic, social, and environmental pillars of sustainability.

### 4.2 TRIPMENTOR project

The TRIPMENTOR project is a game-oriented cultural tourism application designed for the region of Attica. It leverages gamification to enrich visitor experiences by providing personalized routes and promoting user interaction through playful experiences. TRIPMENTOR integrates gamification as both a marketing strategy and a tool for enhancing cultural tourism, demonstrating the potential of gamified experiences to align with the personal needs, interests, and habits of tourists [60].

### 4.3 Gamification in museums

Various examples illustrate how museums globally have adopted gamification to transform visitor experiences. From the Louvre's partnership with Nintendo to create a 3DS audio guide game, to the augmented reality exhibits at the Art and History Museum of Geneva, and the immersive role-playing experiences at Jamtli in Sweden, these cases show how gamification can make museum visits more interactive, educational, and enjoyable. These initiatives not only bolster the social and educational dimensions of museum visits but also encourage repeat attendance and deeper engagement with cultural content [61].

These case studies are just a few examples from the current market implementations. They demonstrate the versatility and effectiveness of gamification in engaging audiences and promoting sustainability within the tourism and cultural sectors. By integrating game elements into experiences, organizations can create memorable, meaningful, and impactful interactions that resonate with visitors' desires for adventure, learning, and environmental stewardship.

## 5. Future directions

As we look towards the future of gamification in luxury tourism, several key trends and advancements are expected to shape its evolution. The convergence of technology, customer experience, and sustainability will drive innovation, offering new ways for luxury tourism providers to engage with their clientele. In the next sections, there are some potential future directions.

### 5.1 Integration with emerging technologies

The use of augmented reality (AR) and virtual reality (VR) will become more sophisticated, offering immersive experiences that can transport guests to virtual environments or enhance their real-world surroundings with digital overlays. These enhancements may provide educational content, historical context, or even fantasy worlds.

Artificial intelligence (AI) will play a crucial role in personalizing gamified experiences. By using data analytics, these technologies will tailor challenges, rewards, and interactions to individual preferences, enhancing the luxury aspect of bespoke service.

### 5.2 Sustainability and gamification

Gamification strategies will increasingly focus on encouraging sustainable tourism practices. They will reward guests for engaging in activities that reduce their environmental impact, such as participating in local conservation efforts or choosing eco-friendly transport options.

Luxury brands will use gamification to educate guests about sustainability issues related to their destinations. Leveraging interactive games and challenges, they aim to raise awareness and foster a deeper connection with the local environment and community.

### 5.3 Enhanced personalization

Future gamification efforts will leverage real-time data to dynamically adjust game content, challenges, and rewards. These adjustments will be based on the guest's location, actions, and even mood, providing a truly personalized and engaging experience.

The Internet of Things (IoT) will enable a seamless gamified experience across various touchpoints. From smart hotel rooms to wearables, it will allow guests to interact with their environment in new and exciting ways.

### 5.4 Social and community engagement

Future gamification approaches will increasingly incorporate elements that encourage social interaction. This could be through competitive leaderboards, collaborative challenges that require teamwork, or shared experiences that connect guests with each other and with local communities.

Encouraging guests to share their experiences on social media and within the game platform itself will not only amplify the reach of gamification campaigns but also provide valuable content and insights for further personalization and community building.

### 5.5 Blockchain and digital rewards

The use of blockchain technology may introduce tokenized rewards. Guests could earn digital tokens that can be redeemed for exclusive experiences, services, or even as part of a loyalty program, adding a new layer of value to the gamification experience.

Blockchain could also enhance the security and transparency of transactions within gamified systems. This would build trust and encourage greater participation.

### 5.6 Regulation and ethical considerations

As gamification relies heavily on data, future developments will need to navigate the complexities of data privacy regulations. This ensures that guest information is collected and used ethically and securely.

Ensuring that gamified experiences are inclusive and accessible to all guests, regardless of age, ability, or digital literacy, will be crucial. It maintains the luxury tourism sector's commitment to excellence and bespoke service.

The future of gamification in luxury tourism is poised for significant growth and innovation. Driven by technological advancements, a focus on sustainability, and the ongoing pursuit of personalized and meaningful guest experiences. As the sector evolves, these trends will likely shape how luxury tourism brands engage with their clientele, offering new opportunities for interaction, engagement, and loyalty.

## 6. Conclusions

The exploration of gamification in luxury tourism reveals a dynamic and evolving field, characterized by innovative applications that enhance guest experiences, promote sustainability, and foster deeper engagement and loyalty. Through the integration of technology, personalized experiences, and sustainable practices, luxury tourism providers can create memorable, engaging, and meaningful interactions with their clients.

The future of gamification in luxury tourism is closely tied to emerging technologies such as augmented reality (AR), virtual reality (VR), artificial intelligence (AI), and the Internet of Things (IoT). These technologies offer novel ways to create immersive and personalized experiences that can set luxury brands apart in a competitive market.

Gamification presents a distinct opportunity to promote sustainable behaviors and practices among tourists. By rewarding eco-friendly actions, luxury tourism providers can contribute to environmental conservation efforts while enhancing the guest experience.

At the heart of successful gamification strategies lies the focus on personalization and engagement. Tailored challenges, rewards, and experiences can deepen guests' connections to the brand and the destination, leading to increased satisfaction and loyalty.

Incorporating social and community elements into gamification strategies can enrich the social experience of travel, connecting guests to one another and to local communities in meaningful ways.

As gamification relies on data collection and digital interactions, ethical considerations around data privacy, security, and inclusivity are paramount. It is essential to ensure that gamified experiences are secure, respectful of privacy, and accessible to all.

Looking forward, the luxury tourism sector must continue to innovate and adapt its gamification strategies to meet the changing needs and expectations of travelers. This includes staying abreast of technological advancements, prioritizing sustainability, and leveraging data analytics for personalized engagement. Furthermore, as the global landscape evolves, particularly in response to challenges such as climate change and digital transformation, luxury tourism providers will need to be agile and responsive in their approach to gamification.

Gamification in luxury tourism represents a potent tool for enhancing the guest experience, driving sustainability, and building brand loyalty. As we look to the future, the successful integration of gamification strategies will hinge on a nuanced understanding of technology, guest expectations, and the broader societal and environmental context. By focusing on innovation, personalization, and sustainability, luxury tourism can continue to offer exceptional experiences that not only delight guests but also contribute positively to the world around us.

## Author details

Ricardo Marcão*, Vasco Santos and Marta Sampaio
ISLA Santarém, Santarém, Portugal

*Address all correspondence to: ricardo.marcao@islasantarem.pt

## References

[1] Deterding S, Dixon D, Khaled R, Nacke L. From game design elements to gamefulness: Defining "gamification". In: Proceedings of the 15th International Academic MindTrek Conference: Envisioning Future Media Environments. Association for Computing Machinery; 2011. pp. 9-15

[2] Hamari J, Koivisto J, Sarsa H. Does gamification work? – A literature review of empirical studies on gamification. In: 2014 47th Hawaii International Conference on System Sciences. 2014. pp. 3025-3034

[3] Tussyadiah IP. A review of research on digitalization in tourism: The emergence of a new paradigm. Journal of Travel Research. 2020;**59**(4):613-628

[4] Pasca MG, Renzi MF, Di Pietro L, Guglielmetti MR. Gamification in tourism and hospitality research in the era of digital platforms: A systematic literature review. Journal of Service Theory and Practice. 2021;**31**(5):691-737

[5] Pasca MG, Renzi MF, Di Pietro L, Guglielmetti Mugion R. Gamification in tourism and hospitality research in the era of digital platforms: a systematic literature review. Journal of Service Theory and Practice. 17 Aug 2021;**31**(5):691-737

[6] Xu F, Weber J, Buhalis D. Gamification in tourism. In: Information and Communication Technologies in Tourism 2014: Proceedings of the International Conference in Dublin, Ireland, January 21-24, 2014. Springer International Publishing; 2013. pp. 525-537

[7] Seaborn K, Fels DI. Gamification in theory and action: A survey. International Journal of Human-Computer Studies. 2015;**74**:14-31

[8] Ryan RM, Deci EL. Self-determination theory and the facilitation of intrinsic motivation, social development, and well-being. American Psychologist. Jan 2000;**55**(1):68

[9] Yeoman I. The changing behaviours of luxury consumption. Journal of Revenue and Pricing Management. 2011;**10**:47-50

[10] Pine BJ, Gilmore JH. The experience economy: Past, present and future. In: Handbook on the experience economy. Edward Elgar Publishing; 30 Sep 2013. pp. 21-44

[11] Tynan C, McKechnie S, Chhuon C. Co-creating value for luxury brands. Journal of Business Research. 2010;**63**(11):1156-1163

[12] Atwal G, Williams A. Luxury brand marketing – The experience is everything! Journal of Brand Management. 2009;**16**(5-6):338-346

[13] Poulsson SHG, Kale SH. The experience economy and commercial experiences. The Marketing Review. 2004;**4**(3):267-277

[14] Sigala M. Collaborative commerce in tourism: Implications for research and industry. Current Issues in Tourism. 2017;**20**(4):346-355

[15] MacCannell D. Staged authenticity: Arrangements of social space in tourist settings. American Journal of Sociology. 1973;**79**(3):589-603

[16] Tung VWS, Ritchie JB. Exploring the essence of memorable tourism

experiences. Annals of Tourism Research. 2011;**38**(4):1367-1386

[17] Loureiro SMC. The role of the rural tourism experience economy in place attachment and behavioral intentions. International Journal of Hospitality Management. 2014;**40**:1-9

[18] Weeden C. Responsible tourist behaviour. Routledge; 15 Aug 2013

[19] Xu F, Buhalis D, Weber J. Serious games and the gamification of tourism. Tourism Management. 2017;**60**:244-256

[20] Hamari J, Koivisto J. Why do people use gamification services? International Journal of Information Management. 2015;**35**(4):419-431

[21] Ritterfeld U, Cody M, Vorderer P, editors. Serious Games: Mechanisms and Effects. Routledge; 10 Sep 2009

[22] Hamari J. Transforming homo economicus into homo ludens: A field experiment on gamification in a utilitarian peer-to-peer trading service. Electronic Commerce Research and Applications. 2013;**12**(4):236-245

[23] Hamid M, Kuppusamy M. Gamification implementation in service marketing: A literature. Electronic Journal of Business & Management. 2017;**2**(1):38-50

[24] Mollick ER, Rothbard N. Mandatory fun: Consent, gamification and the impact of games at work. The Wharton School research paper series. 30 Sep 2014

[25] Xi N, Hamari J. Does gamification satisfy needs? A study on the relationship between gamification features and intrinsic need satisfaction. International Journal of Information Management. 2019;**46**:210-221

[26] Zhang T, Lu C, Kizildag M. Engaging customers in value co-creation or co-destruction online. Journal of Services Marketing. 2017;**31**(1):92-105

[27] Thakur R. Understanding customer engagement and loyalty: A case of mobile devices for shopping. Journal of Retailing and Consumer Services. 2016;**32**:151-163

[28] Khan A, Boroomand F, Webster J, Minocher X. From elements to structures: An agenda for organisational gamification. European Journal of Information Systems. 1 Nov 2020;**29**(6):621-640

[29] Klock AC, Gasparini I, Pimenta MS. User-centered gamification for e-learning systems: A quantitative and qualitative analysis of its application. Interacting with Computers. Sep 2019;**31**(5):425-445

[30] Tussyadiah IP. Toward a theoretical foundation for experience design in tourism. Journal of travel research. Sep 2014;**53**(5):543-564

[31] Lee JJ, Hammer J. Gamification in education: What, how, why bother? Academic Exchange Quarterly. 2013;**15**(2)

[32] Kim AJ, Ko E. Do social media marketing activities enhance customer equity? An empirical study of luxury fashion brand. Journal of Business Research. 2015;**65**(10):1480-1486

[33] Tussyadiah IP, Pesonen J. Impacts of peer-to-peer accommodation use on travel patterns. Journal of Travel Research. 2016;**55**(8):1022-1040

[34] Basterfield L, Gardner L, Reilly JK, Pearce MS, Parkinson KN, Adamson AJ, et al. Can't play, won't play: Longitudinal changes in perceived barriers to participation in sports clubs across

the child–adolescent transition. BMJ Open Sport & Exercise Medicine. 1 Mar 2016;**2**(1):e000079

[35] Tene O, Polonetsky J. Privacy in the age of big data: A time for big decisions. Stanford Law Review Online. 2012;**64**:63

[36] Deterding S. Gamification: Designing for motivation. Interactions. 2012;**19**(4):14-17

[37] Weaver DB. Ecotourism as mass tourism: Contradiction or reality? Cornell Hospitality Quarterly. 2011;**52**(2):247-257

[38] Huang WH, Soman D. A Practitioner's guide to gamification of education. In: Research Report Series Behavioural Economics in Action, Rotman School of Management. University of Toronto; 2013

[39] Giovanella F. Bibliography: Conflicting Rights in Balance. In: Copyright and Information Privacy. Edward Elgar Publishing; 29 Dec 2017. pp. 316-348

[40] Hofstede G. Culture's Consequences: International Differences in Work-Related Values. Sage; 1984

[41] Guttentag DA. Virtual reality: Applications and implications for tourism. Tourism Management. 2010;**31**(5):637-651

[42] Hsu CL, Chen MC. How does gamification improve user experience? An empirical investigation on the antecedences and consequences of user experience and its mediating role. Technological Forecasting and Social Change. 2018;**132**:118-129

[43] Weaver DB. Can sustainable tourism survive climate change? Journal of Sustainable Tourism. 2011;**19**(1):5-15

[44] Zichermann G, Cunningham C. Gamification by Design: Implementing Game Mechanics in Web and Mobile Apps. O'Reilly Media, Inc.; 25 Jul 2011

[45] Deci EL, Ryan RM. Intrinsic Motivation and Self-Determination in Human Behavior. Springer Science & Business Media; 29 Jun 2013

[46] Csikszentmihalyi M, Csikzentmihaly M. Flow: The Psychology of Optimal Experience. New York: Harper and Row; Mar 1990

[47] Ajzen I. The theory of planned behavior. Organizational Behavior and Human Decision Processes. 1991;**50**(2):179-211

[48] Prochaska JO, DiClemente CC. Stages and processes of self-change of smoking: Toward an integrative model of change. Journal of Consulting and Clinical Psychology. 1983;**51**(3):390-395

[49] Vargo SL, Lusch RF. Evolving to a new dominant logic for marketing. Journal of Marketing. 2004;**68**(1):1-17

[50] Jain S, Mishra S, Saxena G. Luxury customer's motivations to adopt gamification. Marketing Intelligence & Planning. 13 Mar 2023;**41**(2):156-170

[51] Gebauer H, Pütz F, Fischer T, Fleisch E. Service orientation of organizational structures. Journal of Relationship Marketing. 22 May 2009;**8**(2):103-126

[52] Parasuraman A, Zeithaml VA, Berry LL. A conceptual model of service quality and its implications for future research. Journal of Marketing. 1985;**49**(4):41-50

[53] Beaujean M, Davidson J, Madge S. The 'moment of truth' in customer

service. McKinsey Quarterly. Feb 2006;**1**:62-73

[54] Christopher M, Payne A, Ballantyne D. Relationship Marketing. Routledge; 17 Jun 2013

[55] Davis FD. Perceived usefulness, perceived ease of use, and user acceptance of information technology. MIS Quarterly. 1989;**13**(3):319-340

[56] Venkatesh V, Morris MG, Davis GB, Davis FD. User acceptance of information technology: Toward a unified view. MIS Quarterly. 2003;**27**(3):425-478

[57] Rogers EM, Singhal A, Quinlan MM. Diffusion of innovations. In: An Integrated Approach to Communication Theory and Research. Routledge; 8 Apr 2014. pp. 432-448

[58] Freeman RE. Strategic Management: A Stakeholder Approach. Cambridge University Press; 11 Mar 2010

[59] Negruşa AL, Toader V, Sofică A, Tutunea MF, Rus RV. Exploring gamification techniques and applications for sustainable tourism. Sustainability. 2015;**7**(8):11160-11189

[60] Roinioti E, Pandia E, Konstantakis M, Skarpelos Y. Gamification in tourism: A design framework for the TRIPMENTOR project. Digital. 2022;**2**(2):191-205

[61] Sarker MT, Economou D, Eardley A. Doctoral colloquium—treasure hunt AR for enhancing visiting experience in cultural sites. In: 2022 8th International Conference of the Immersive Learning Research Network (iLRN). IEEE; 30 May 2022. pp. 1-3

Chapter 4

# Online and Mobile-Assisted Language Learning

*Omnia Ibrahim Mohamed and Omar Al-Jadaan*


## Abstract

Online language classes and mobile-assisted language learning applications (Apps) are non-traditional methods of education that differ from traditional classes, which involve face-to-face instruction and teacher-led lessons. Web or mobile-assisted language learning applications cater to the changing world, making them convenient and affordable for those with limited time. These applications can be used at the learners' convenience, making them a qualitative leap in the field of language learning. There is a world full of language applications some of which are dedicated to the education of the English Language as the Global language and others have many languages to learn. In the explorations of language applications, the Google Bundle is one of the best for online classes as it is the most comprehensive bundle and Duolingo is the best language application, if we considered the increasing number of its downloads and its continuously increasing revenue. Most of the applications have free and Pro or Premium features, and some only offer a free trial of one lesson or a seven-day trial. Each application has different teaching methods; some use gamification, interactive exercises, communicative approach, spaced repetition, contextual learning, audio-visual learning, and personalization. Moreover, most of the applications employ Artificial intelligence (AI) for immediate feedback.


**Keywords:** online language learning, Google bundle, mobile-assisted language learning (MALL) applications, Duolingo, cake language learning application, Babbel, hello English, artificial intelligence (AI), gamification, personalization, audio-visual learning

## 1. Introduction

The Internet and mobile technology have practically infiltrated every facet of our life. All over the globe, everyone is surfing the internet and its applications using their cell phones, tablets, laptops, or desktops, especially students at all levels of education.

For a long time, technology has mastered the area of education. Emails, university management systems (UMS), and WhatsApp are all methods that educational institutions use to communicate with their students. There are WhatsApp groups for each subject as well as for students of the same academic year. Instructors or teachers may also join these groups to facilitate interaction with their students. Learners have been introduced to information technology, which has changed their learning styles and processes. Net Generation learners believe that employing technology in the classroom is vital as the majority of them have benefited from Internet resources in their education.

Hulme (2020) explained that Mobile devices can serve as a link between in-class and out-of-class learning. When learning occurs outside of the classroom, it is frequently outside the teacher's grasp and control. This may be regarded as a danger, but it is also a chance to revitalize and rethink present teaching and learning practices. For several reasons, mobile learning appeals to a wide spectrum of people. The next generation of mobile learning is anticipated to be more pervasive, which implies that there will be smart systems for digital learning everywhere. Mobile learning is demonstrating its ability to meet real learner demands at the place of need and to provide more flexible language learning methods [1].

Due to the COVID-19 pandemic lockdown in 2020, all educational institutions recognized that everything was different than it used to be. The benefits of electronic education have risen to the forefront. Suddenly, everyone started working virtually. People involved in training, teaching, and higher education had to employ remote access to content that they were totally or partially ignorant about. They began to figure out a method to interact even though they were all in the same geographical spot. All learners, anywhere, were required to participate in online learning. Both students and teachers had to adjust in the absence of live face-to-face classes. They were all quickly instructed to use virtual educational platforms like Google Classroom, Google Meet, Google Docs, and Google Forms, as well as conventional communication tools like email and WhatsApp. As a result, the whole educational environment has evolved substantially as this was a worldwide event, not a local or national one. Some disciplines presented difficulties for both students and teachers since it was difficult for them to figure out how are they going to teach without classroom contact. Amongst these disciplines was a language like English, although several English courses, such as the IGCSE, SAT, or even general English language classes, were previously offered virtually, not the regular daily classes.

Nevertheless, many features of virtual or online teaching and learning had to be extensively investigated to determine the efficiency of various online techniques in teaching the four skills of any language (reading, writing, listening, and speaking), as well as presentation skills. WhatsApp, email, and mostly Google educational tools were employed in educating and interacting with students. Each of these educational applications served an important purpose in the process of online English instruction. Aside from WhatsApp, email, and UMS, Google applications played the most significant part at the time of the pandemic up till now.

On the other hand, there are other language tools for self-education in any second language. This is called mobile-assisted language education in which any learner can self-educate him/herself without having to join regular classes whether it be online or onsite. These applications have become very popular recently as they teach language according to the learner's convenience. Anyone can use these language applications anytime and in any place. They can even use it whilst commuting from one place to the other or whilst waiting for any service to be accomplished or even whilst waiting for their turn in a queue.

These mobile applications can teach learners all four skills required to learn a second language. They all use the communicative approach which is a language learning methodology that emphasizes learning through real-life communication, focuses on developing learners' ability to use language in a meaningful and authentic context, and engages them to practise listening, speaking reading, and writing in a natural situation. Most of these applications use artificial Intelligence (AI). But, each application has a different method of teaching.

Some applications use gamification which is the incorporation of game elements and mechanisms such as points, badges, leaderboards, and challenges into non-game contexts like the education method. That resembles mobile games and gives rewards (XPs) and the learner has lives that can decrease when the learner gives wrong answers until they expire and the learner has to wait for a refill. Most of the applications also use "Contextual Learning" which focuses on understanding information within its relevant context or setting, emphasizing the importance of grasping the meaning and application of concepts by considering the circumstances in which they are used. For example, context related to job interviews, travels, family...etc.

Other applications rely on videos and podcasts from movies or famous sitcoms that help to enrich the vocabulary of learners. Others redirect learners to recorded classes on YouTube channels by professional language tutors and few applications allow users to book live classes with tutors of their choice, depending on the reviews of previous learners.

This chapter will cover both types of language learning. It will discuss online language learning by professional lecturers, which can also be through the use of laptops, desktops or mobiles. It will also discuss the self-learning of language by discussing the most renowned language learning applications and attempting to compare them to the rest of the less popular applications.

## 2. The Google bundle

### 2.1 Google meet

Google Meet is a very important Google application in education, in general, and in language learning, in particular. This program establishes a live connection between the teacher and the students. The teachers may meet with the students in real time and share a computer screen with them to see demonstrations, files, presentations, images, and other media. They may even record the lecture or class for the students to watch later if they like. When the recording is finished, the teachers can immediately share the recorded lesson with the students using Google Drive. By using Google Meet, the four skills of a language can be learned virtually and easily without having to go to a language centre.

### 2.2 Google docs

Google Docs, one of Google's educational tools, is a very important tool in education. It is free and easily accessible. They are safe online applications that automatically save data with a low probability of loss. Students can use their gadgets to access, generate, compose, modify, or share documents. Students can also add links, photographs, illustrations, or artwork to their Google Document before sharing it or saving it as a PDF file or Microsoft Word.

### 2.3 Google forms

With Google Forms, teachers can simply collect and categorize content, as well as create custom questionnaires, forms, and quizzes. After students complete the Google form, their replies are shown as a brief overview or in an independent spreadsheet to illustrate specifics. Google Forms, documents, and spreadsheets are constantly updated and retained on the World Wide Web.

### 2.4 Google drive

Other programs that enhance the teaching and learning processes are included in Google applications. They provide a means for teachers' courses and activities to be shared. Google Drive is one of Google's most important educational applications. The teacher can upload large files and provide links for students to share. Teachers can also make a roster of the students they teach and assign them to groups.

### 2.5 Google classroom

Another educational program that is used for online teaching is Google Classroom, through which the teachers can create classes and ask students to participate in them. After the teacher creates the class, he/she may upload lessons, quizzes, and assignments in any format, such as video, audio, PowerPoint, Word, or PDF. Once the teacher sets up a class, a Class Drive folder is automatically established to receive students' work. Furthermore, teachers may engage with their students via the "stream", where they can exchange postings and schedule communications. After the pandemic, the dependence on mobile applications increased tremendously and virtual education using applications prevailed. Pachler, Cook, and Bachmair (2010) stated that Mobile-Assisted Language Learning (MALL), a subset of M(mobile)-learning, is a rapidly growing field with important implications for teaching English with Technology [2].

Therefore, as Mohamed (2021) stated these Applications can be used as successful online learning instruments and can be implemented rapidly to enhance blended learning. Using Google Meet, Google Classroom, Google Docs, and other supporting internet applications like WhatsApp, email, and mobile phones, had significant effects on delivering quality English language courses and achieving the learning outcomes required [3]. This has been proven successful as many of the renowned language centres like the British Council are now offering online as well as onsite courses for the learners to choose from according to their convenience.

## 3. Mobile-assisted language education

Away from learning a language within the educational or academic system, in today's increasingly globalized world, self-learning a new language for purposes other than academic purposes has become a valuable skill, whether for personal growth, career development or increased cultural awareness. The benefits of becoming bilingual or multilingual are undeniable. Recognizing this need and the increasing availability of mobile technology has contributed to a growth in mobile-assisted language learning, in which learners can study a second language (L2) autonomously at any time or place. Moreover, the idea of learning a language anytime, anywhere with the use of mobile devices can motivate learners and encourage them to take responsibility for their own learning process, which in turn can make them feel that they have authority over the process [4].

Most language learning applications are "freemium". This term is a combination of the words "free" and "premium", and refers to a pricing model in which a basic good or service is offered free of charge, but additional features or services, are available for purchase at a cost that enhances the capabilities of the free version of the software. Other applications offer a free trial of one lesson or a seven-day trial and then the user has to pay to start the process of learning.

There are several evaluations of language learning applications, but each evaluation has different criteria. Some of the evaluations are restricted to a certain area or a certain group. For example, Forbes's evaluation is restricted to the USA only, and CNN's evaluations are also restricted to the viewers of CNN. Yet, the number of downloads can also reflect which application is more popular than the other worldwide.

### 3.1 Duolingo

According to Forbes, *Duolingo* is the "Best Free Language Lessons". It is indeed one of the best mobile-assisted language applications. Duolingo and Cake applications are on top regarding downloads, as each application has reached 100M+ downloads. The application offers 40 languages for free. It is an application designed to make language learning enjoyable and simple, and it has proven to be very successful in this goal. This is proven by the chart below where Duolingo's downloads have increased from 120 to 673M in 8 years. Moreover, the number of daily active users is constantly increasing (**Figure 1**).

In Duolingo, the users are invited to submit information about their present language competence level and to define their language learning objectives after installing the application. Based on this information, Duolingo generates a customized curriculum that is suited to the needs of the particular user. This personalized learning technique results in a more efficient and effective learning experience. Personalization is education tailoring to meet the individual needs, preferences, and learning styles of each student. This approach creates a more relevant and engaging learning environment that suits every learner.

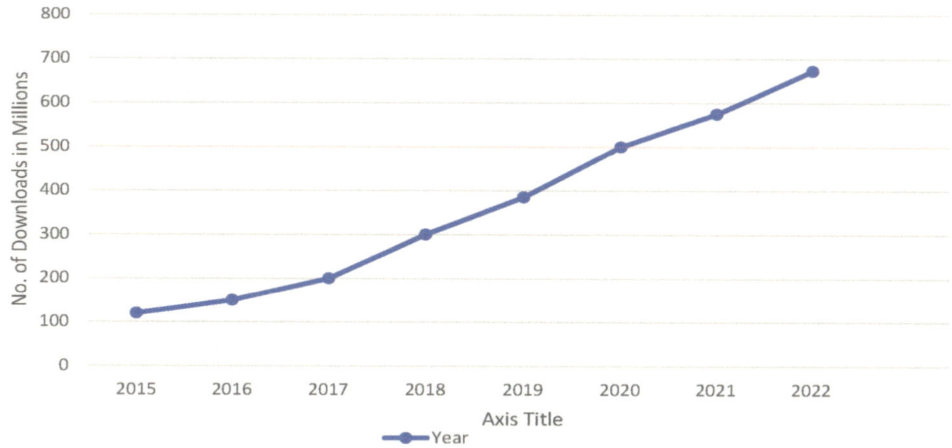


**Figure 1.**
*Duolingo downloads from 2015 to 2022.*

One of the key features of Duolingo is its gamification approach used in language learning. To motivate users to finish lessons and progress through the course, the program incorporates a point system (XPs). Users receive points for completing lessons and may compete with their friends to see who can gain the most points. This gamification method is particularly effective, since it keeps the users interested and motivated. The user may only be asked to pay if he/she wants to buy extra lives, like in any mobile game. According to Duolingo's website, a research conducted by the City University of New York estimated that 34 hours of Duolingo study was similar to one semester of college-level language learning. This great accomplishment demonstrates the application's usefulness in assisting users in learning a new language. Duolingo offers 95 courses accessible in 38 languages and has over 500 million registered subscribers, of whom 37 million are active at least once every month.

Loewen, et.al (2019) conducted a study that examined the semester-long learning experiences and outcomes of nine people who use Duolingo to learn Turkish. At the end of the research, the participants' skills were improved on second language (L2) assessments, and the results demonstrated a positive, moderate link between the amount of time spent on Duolingo and the achievements. In terms of their experiences, participants generally rated Duolingo's flexibility and gamification components favorably; nevertheless, they also expressed variety in motivation to study and dissatisfaction with teaching materials [5].

Most of the reviews on Duolingo praise it as one of the best motivating language applications due to its gamification method and competitive mode, its content and its daily goals, basics and sentence structure learning method. Yet, the basic explanation of grammar is missing and there is no method to correct what is wrong. Moreover, in the competitive mode, you cannot participate without a subscription as it leaves much to be desired by the non-subscribers. The advertisements (ads.) are also present in most of the applications, but they are not disruptive according to most of the reviews.

### 3.2 Cake: Learn English and Korean

Similarly, **Cake – Learn English and Korean** is a very popularly downloaded application that exceeded 100 Million downloads and that has very good reviews from customers. Yet, despite its popularity, it only offers two languages—English and Korean. This fact shows that it is a very successful application since it offers only two languages and still, it is one of the top-rated applications. Moreover, being originally a South Korean application, it is not only popular in Asia Pacific Region but also in Europe and the United States. The below chart shows the downloads of Cake worldwide from the 1st quarter of 2020 to 2nd quarter of 2022 (**Figure 2**).

This application has a free and a plus version, and like Duolingo, it has the same gaming path where the users move along as they finish lessons. Cake relies mostly on popular videos. It teaches certain expressions, sentences, or idioms by showing them on movie clips from famous movies or sitcoms like "Friends" or cartoons like "The Simpsons", which make the learning experience more fun and enjoyable. This provides the users with an innovative and effective way to learn languages. It stands out from other language learning platforms due to its unique approach and comprehensive features.

Yet, Cake does not check the level of knowledge of the user as Duolingo does. It immediately starts with lessons that are not specified to a certain level. The application has a user-friendly interface which makes language learning enjoyable and easily

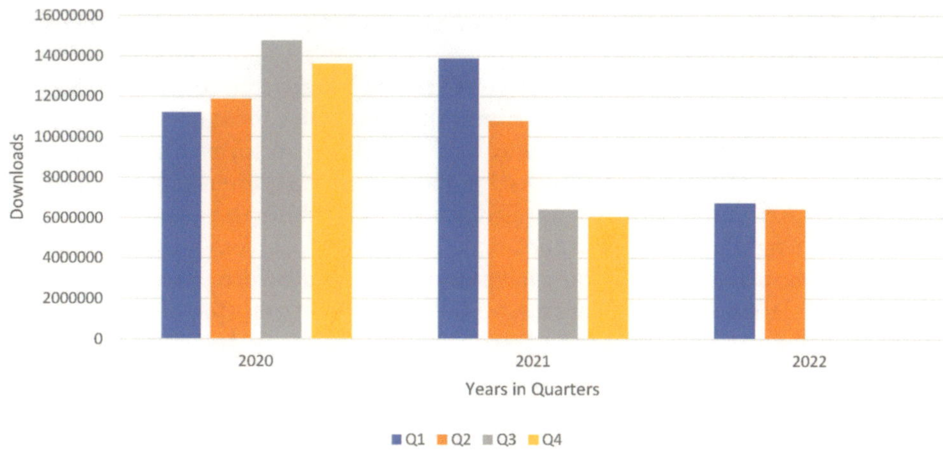


**Figure 2.**
*Downloads of language learning app Cake worldwide from 1st quarter 2020 to 2nd quarter 2022.*

accessible. It also has clear navigation and an intuitive design that even beginners can use without feeling overwhelmed.

Moreover, Cake also uses the gamification techniques, like Duolingo, to motivate and engage users turning language learning into a fun and addictive experience. The progress of learners is tracked through a visually appealing path allowing users to see their achievements and areas for improvement at a glance. As previously mentioned, another standout feature of Cake is its interactive activities designed to enhance language retention of educational content and practical application. Interactive activities or exercises require active participation from learners often using digital platforms.

The application provides a wide range of exercises, including vocabulary, quizzes, grammar drills, listening comprehension exercises, and speaking practice. Yet, some of the reviews and practices are not accessible except for the plus subscribers. The free subscribers are directed to subscribe to selected YouTube channels where there are language teachers who give classes on certain topics from which the users can select according to their needs and preferences. Moreover, there are also some tips for language in the form of short reels that are partially accessible to free subscribers. Through its diverse content offerings, users can choose from a wide range of topics, including business, travel, culture, and entertainment, ensuring that they are learning vocabulary and skills relevant to their interests and future goals. These classes and interactive activities help users develop all aspects of language proficiency, ensuring a well-rounded language learning experience. Therefore, it accommodates different learning styles and preferences.

To further support users in their language learning journey, Cake incorporates a vibrant community of fellow language enthusiasts. The application allows users to see the progress of other learners, which creates an atmosphere of competition and challenge that encourages users. Furthermore, Cake offers audio and video lessons allowing users to practise their listening and comprehension skills with authentic language materials to cater to busy individuals that involve using auditory and visual cues to enhance learning, and using multimedia to engage learners. It also provides a flexible learning experience with its offline mode, since users can access their lessons and activities without an internet connection making it possible to learn on the go, even during commutes or whilst traveling. In addition, the application offers bite-sized lessons allowing users to squeeze in language learning during small pockets of free time.

Yet, the drawbacks of this application were that it is restricted to only two languages (English and Korean), and sometimes there is a voice recognition problem in the speaking skills practice no matter how loud and clear you speak, and sometimes it glitches and does not record the voice; that most of the customers complained of. Moreover, in the speaking part, the application keeps marking the mistakes in yellow without correcting the wrong pronunciation. The second problem is that sometimes it quizzes the learners on lessons they have never reviewed before. Another complaint is that there are lessons that are not free, and of course, the most popular complaint of all users in all the applications is the advertisements that always interrupt the learning session.

Some reviews claim that this application is far better than Duolingo and that it is more interactive as it offers a wider range of interactive lessons that are very engaging and well-structured. Moreover, the content is diverse, covering various topics such as vocabulary, grammar, listening, and speaking. The aforementioned bite-sized lessons are also well-praised by the users as this gives them a chance to improve their pronunciation and practise what they have already learned. Another praise was for the type of videos used, as they are taken from the media and are fun to watch. The application also scores the quizzes like video games and sends new phrases and reminders throughout the day.

### 3.3 Babbel: Language learning

Another prominent application is *Babbel*, which is an esteemed language learning platform operated by Babbel GmbH, a renowned company that started in 2007 located in Berlin, Germany. In 2013, it expanded to the USA and continues to thrive in its innovative journey.

Babbel is ranked after Duolingo and Cake with 50M+ downloads. It is also ranked in Forbes as the "Best Language Learning App Overall" and it is the winner of the 2020 IELA E-Learning Award in the category of mobile-assisted learning. Millions of individuals across the world have downloaded the application, which is accessible on both the Android and iOS platforms. It was designed to help users learn a new language. The application offers courses in English and 13 different languages, including Spanish, French, German, Italian, Portuguese, Russian, Turkish, Dutch, Polish, Indonesian, Norwegian, Danish, and Swedish. On the application, it is stated that "The Babbel method is backed by researchers at Yale University. According to research, 75% of learners accomplish their goal with Babbel".

Babbel made a revenue of €198 Million in 2021. It had some losses over the years from 2015 to 2023, but it has overcome these losses. In "The Business of Applications" website, the revenues of Babbel and Duolingo are compared in the following graph (**Figure 3**).

From the chart, it is evident that the profits of Duolingo's revenue exceeded Babbel in 2022. But what is surprising is that Babbel's revenues have exceeded Duolingo from 2017 till mid-2020. Then Duolingo boomed in 2021 and 2022.

The application starts by asking learners about their native language. Just as the learners choose their native language, the language of the application changes to the native language chosen. Yet, many important languages are not available, like Arabic, Russian, or Chinese. Therefore, many people who would like to use the application may not use it because of this defect. On the other hand, Babbel has an advantage

DOI: http://dx.doi.org/10.5772/intechopen.1003054

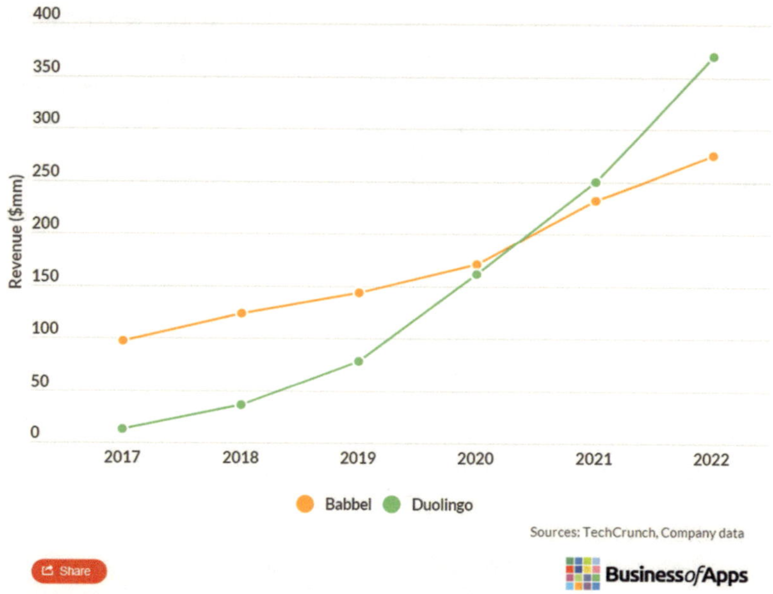


**Figure 3.**
*Revenues of Babbel and Duolingo from 2017 till 2022 [6]*

that is not available in Duolingo; it classifies the languages available according to the dialects. For example, it has British English and American English or Spanish Spain and Latin Spanish. Therefore, the users can choose the dialect they prefer.

Babbel does not test the users' proficiency level at the beginning. It just asks the users about their knowledge of the target language, and they have to choose between "not much", "some", or "a lot". Yet, there is an optional placement test for the user to use according to their preference. It also inquires about the reason for learning the language and the time they want to allocate for learning to tailor the course according to the preference of the users. This is an advantage of Babbel as it allows personalized learning. The application employs a unique algorithm that determines the user's learning style and tailors the courses accordingly. In other words, the program will deliver lessons that are personalized to the users' specific requirements and learning preferences. In addition, there are Live Courses where the users can book a specific teacher, and for certain languages, podcasts are also available as an additional resource. Yet, the amount of content present in each language may vary.

Podcasts in Babbel are a very unique feature that was noticed by researchers. Sporn, Chanter, and Meehan (2020) wrote an article that describes the pedagogical method and expertise behind Babbel's podcasts along with some best practices for creating effective audio-based learning experiences. They stated that Babbel's podcast library provides creative audio-learning experiences for language learning and cultural enrichment. Users find the strategies used, such as sound design, contextual assistance, speech tempo, and duration, valuable for beginners. Over 90% of respondents to a survey found the level appropriate for them, and the detailed advice provided was welcomed. The success of this approach for beginners is evident, and Babbel plans to explore new routes for authentic audio and explore its potential for other language learners [7].

Yet, Babbel's courses do not rely on gamification in progress, but there is a section for games where the learners can play fun word games that enhance their vocabulary and conversation skills. In general, The content found in Babbel is valuable and poses a good level of difficulty, accommodating individuals with varying degrees of proficiency. However, unlike Duolingo, it is not free. Nevertheless, its cost is reasonable and makes it attainable for a diverse pool of learners. Users are presented with the opportunity to select from an assortment of subscription options, such as monthly and yearly plans. Customers may cancel their memberships at any moment; also, the application provides a free trial period that allows users to test out the program before committing to a subscription.

Moreover, the program includes tasks and quizzes to help users reinforce their knowledge outside of the application. For example, the application includes a vocabulary trainer that allows users to practise their vocabulary on the go as well as a speech recognition feature that allows users to practise their pronunciation and speaking skills. Moreover, the application includes a feature that allows users to connect with native speakers of the language they are learning, which allows them to practise their language skills in a real-world setting. Furthermore, hint popups or instructional blurbs are particularly beneficial for beginners seeking guidance and ensuring an effective learning experience.

However, it is essential to improve the visual layout of the topics and lessons that have been completed. This will enhance readability and help users navigate through the material more effectively. Moreover, there are also problems related to the voice recognition feature and the same problem, that is mentioned in other applications, of not correcting the pronunciation is evident too. Another drawback is that the users cannot go back to redo previous lessons, yet there is a review feature. Some users claimed that the web version is better than the mobile application, especially in the voice recognition feature and the rapid loading of the lessons, as loading the lessons on the application sometimes requires several trials. There were also complaints regarding the grammatical content being detailed and complex. Spending a lot of time on some grammar topics or complex grammatical structures at the early stage of learning can be demotivating.

### 3.4 Hello English: Learn English

*Hello English* is another 50M+ downloads application. As it is evident from the name, this application is not multilingual. It only focuses on the English language. And the fact that it only focuses on English and has 50M+ downloads reflects the importance of learning the English language globally as well as the success of the application in attracting this number of learners of English. This app was awarded Google's Editor's Choice 2017, 2018 and Google's best app for 2016 as well as being chosen as "India's Best Mobile App" for 2017 by IAMAI (Internet and Mobile Association of India).

Once the learners register, they are asked about their learning objective; whether they want to learn English for travel, for a better career, for a certain competitive exam. etc. Then the application asks about the type of learner if he/she is a student, college graduate, retired, working...etc. As with most of the applications, there are two versions. The learner is asked if he/she wants the limited version or the Pro version. The Pro Version has more options and facilities than the limited one. But the learner can use the limited version successfully, as it is also a good version. The Pro version has unlimited access to all live speaking sessions and 100+ hours of interactive courses. Moreover, all the lessons are unlocked offline and the app is ad-free then with no interruptions.

What is different about this application is that it has a "Helpline". This feature is like WhatsApp, where you can ask your teacher questions and every day the teacher sends material on the Helpline for the learner. This material can be a list of vocabulary words, grammatical instructions, a small reading comprehension passage followed by questions, some idioms, or sentences used on special occasions or in certain situations ...etc.

Learners have a new lesson every day in which they can earn coins by answering questions related to certain selected topics. They can either claim the coins or double them up. The questions are all translated into the native language that the learner selected at the beginning of the sign-up. There are also hanging comments that appear to give the learner grammatical or spelling tips related to a certain question. In the pro subscription, you can go through your mistakes immediately after finishing the questions. This feature is called "Smart Revision". There is also a Gold Plan, where learners can have live classes with English experts.

The application tackles the four skills of English in a very interesting and interactive manner. Learners can challenge and play with other learners and participate in multiplayer challenge tournaments and earn awards. Yet, there are some drawbacks and one of them is the fact that the application runs in the native language of the learner like Babbel. The application offers only 14 languages and half of them are Indian dialects like Punjabi, Tamil, Urdu, Nepali, Malayalam, Malay, and Hindi. Hence, if the learner's native language is not there, he/she will not be able to use the application. Some learners complained that in live classes, the teachers do not translate the slides in their native language. Yet, this translation method is not professional, as according to many linguists and teachers in this field, when there is no translation in language classes, more class communication and action are involved because the teacher tries to use all the facilities and all the skills he/she has to deliver the information. In this process, though it may take a longer time, whatever is being taught lingers in the head of the learners and the vocabulary is retained for a long time without the help of bilingualism. This is totally the opposite when translation is used because when students acquire something easily, it goes as easily as it is acquired [8]. Otherwise, nearly all the reviews are positive except for rare cases of crashes or slow loading of pictures.

## 4. Other mobile-assisted language applications

Now that we have discussed the highest-rated language applications regarding their features, advantages and disadvantages, below is a glimpse at other mobile-assisted language applications and the main features and teaching methodologies used by each application. These applications are with lower than 11M downloads and are also widely used.

### 4.1 Rosetta stone: Learn languages (10M+)

Uses an immersion learning method without learning implementing a contextual multimedia approach (images, text, and audio) to develop language skills.

### 4.2 Busuu-learn languages (10M+)

Uses a combination of lessons, exercises, and social interaction for developing interactive writing, speaking, and listening skills. For correction of writing exercises, peer review is applied.

### 4.3 Memrise: Speak a new language (10M+)

Focuses on vocabulary acquisition, along with spaced repetition technique for better retention. User-generated content for a variety of languages [9]. This is called the "Spaced Repetition" learning technique which involves reviewing and practising information at increasing intervals over time, in order to optimize memory retention by revisiting content just before forgetting starts to occur. This technique is employed in several language learning applications.

### 4.4 ELSA: AI learn and speak English (10M+)

Improves English language speaking through AI-powered technology, using speech recognition to correct pronunciation [10].

### 4.5 Lingodeer-learn languages (10M+)

Offers interactive lessons for Asian languages as well as Spanish, French, and German with a focus on reading, listening, and speaking, where the cultural context is integrated.

### 4.6 BBC learning English (10M+)

Offers audio-video content for improving English language skills, using News and stories to enhance listening and comprehension.

### 4.7 Mondly learn 33 languages (10M+)

Offers interactive lessons with an emphasis on vocabulary building, phrases, and conversations, using gamification elements as Augmented Reality features for engagement.

### 4.8 ABA English (10M+)

Video-based lessons representing real-life scenarios, supported by grammar and vocabulary exercises for comprehension learning [11].

### 4.9 Improve English: Vocabulary grammar (5M+)

Builds English language vocabulary through games, and quizzes with an emphasis on building a strong word base. It focuses on improving vocabulary retention and usage.

### 4.10 Beelinguapp language audiobook (5M+)

A bilingual reading side-by-side in two languages that emphasizes improving reading skills through stories. Learners read and listen in Spanish, German, French, and more.

### 4.11 Learn English grammar (1M+)

An only English application operated by the British Council. It is grammar-focused to improve English language skills, lessons, and quizzes covering various grammar topics.

### 4.12 Andy-English speaking bot (1M+)

An English language learning app through chatbot conversation, with emphasis on daily interaction and vocabulary building.

### 4.13 Pimsleur: Language learning (1M+)

An audio-based application with emphasis on pronunciation and speaking that uses the gradual introduction of new vocabulary and concepts. It also has videos that use the repetitive method to build vocabulary.

### 4.14 Lingbe: Practice languages (1M+)

A language exchange application for speaking practice with a native speaker.

### 4.15 Bright English for beginners (1M+)

A vocabulary builder and grammar-focused app for learning languages based on personalized lessons customized to learner proficiency.

### 4.16 LingQ-learn 42 languages (1M+)

A reading-focused app with authentic content in various languages, building vocabulary through context and repetition. It also employs videos, podcasts, and web articles.

### 4.17 IELTS prep app (1M+)

An English application that is empowered by the British Council to develop English language skills for the IELTS proficiency test.

### 4.18 FluentU: Learn language videos (500K)

Uses real-world video with interactive subtitles supported by contextual learning and exposure to authentic language usage.

### 4.19 UTalk – Learn 150+ languages (500K)

Focuses on vocabulary building with emphasis on practical phrases, using quizzes and interactive exercises for reinforcement. Also, it focuses on real-world conversation and context along with audio recordings by native speakers for pronunciation.

### 4.20 Lingopie: Language learning (100K+)

Uses language learning through TV series and movie subtitles in both targeted and native languages for contextual learning.

### 4.21 Talk English learning (100K+)

A language exchange app for speaking practice with native speakers. It also has free English lessons.

### 4.22 LillyPad English learning app (10K)

Uses interactive lessons along with audiovisual content for improving listening and speaking skills. It builds vocabulary through engaging exercises and quizzes.

### 4.23 Mosalingua

There are several language applications empowered by Mosalingua. There are separate applications for French, Spanish, English, Portuguese, German, Chinese, Japanese, Russian, and Italian. There are also applications for TOEFL, TOEIC, Medical English, and Business English. In language applications, the app uses flashcard-based vocabulary and phrases builder, using context and spaced repetition for improving retention.

## 5. Revenue of mobile-assisted language applications

From the above, it is clear that the use of the Internet and Mobile applications to learn new languages is booming. There is no doubt about that as it is also rewarding to its creators. These applications bring revenues in Billions. The below chart shows the annual revenues from 2016 to 2021, which shows a noticeable kick in 2020 and 2021, may be this is due to the Pandemic of the Corona Virus that started in 2019–2020 and since then the inclination to use the internet and mobile has increased tremendously (**Figure 4**).

The fact that this business is flourishing is due to the fact that using language learning applications has several benefits.

### 5.1 Advantages and key benefits of mobile-assisted language applications

1. Save Time and Learn Anytime: You can learn whenever you want anytime.

2. Learn at your own speed from anywhere: You may study in a relaxed setting and at your own leisure.

3. You have the freedom to select any language and course: You can select the language and course that best meet your demands.

4. Language learning apps are inexpensive: Compared to conventional language classes, language learning apps are frequently more economical.

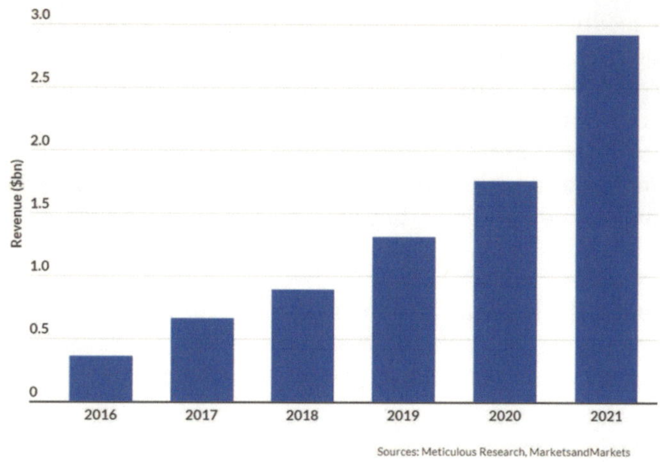


**Figure 4.**
*Annual revenue of language learning apps from 2016 to 2021 [12].*

5. You may develop at your own pace without being constrained by the rules of typical language education.

6. You can take pleasure in the educational process: Many language learning applications make use of multimedia, audio and video, or interactive methods.

7. Availability of In-person lessons with an instructor in some applications including in-person lessons with a teacher, offering individualized teaching.

8. You can begin speaking right away as many language learning applications place an emphasis on speaking abilities straight away, assisting you in beginning to use the language.

## 6. Artificial intelligence and mobile-assisted language applications

It has been observed that employing AI to teach languages is very successful. Due to its ability to examine grammar and identify speech patterns, AI is extremely useful when working with languages. Language learning is advancing substantially as a result of AI algorithms and their use of large data. The demands of each learner may be met when employing AI to learn a new language. Educators can get important information on students' skills and learning preferences. This data can forecast future performance and open the door to personalized learning when properly analysed. AI technology solutions are an effective way to support students as they progress in their language acquisition. The ability to customize the learning process is one of the main advantages of AI. Finding a method that works for everyone in a class of learners is very difficult, yet, the demands of each learner may be met when employing AI to learn a new language.

Using mobile English language learning applications with AI has many benefits. Amongst the key advantages are:

1. Immediate feedback: The AI language learning applications can instantly evaluate tests and even essays after they are uploaded, pointing out errors and recommending corrections. Thus, allowing the learner to identify and correct mistakes promptly, facilitating faster learning and improvement.

2. Increases motivation for learning: Students may choose their own objectives, study whenever and wherever they choose, and use a personalized curriculum to master the language.

3. Language bots: The latest advancement in language learning is language bots. The student only needs to start a discussion with the language bot to receive feedback, advice, and corrections.

4. Adaptive learning: Based on a learner's development and comprehension, AI may modify the course material and delivery method.

5. Natural Language Processing: By employing Natural Language Processing (NLP) to examine learners' pronunciation, grammar, and vocabulary1, AI can improve language acquisition.

6. Assessment and analytics: AI provides automated tests and analytics to assist educators or administrators in monitoring students' progress and locating potential areas for performance or content improvement.

The above points about the importance of AI in language learning were reflected in a study by Mukhallafi (2020) in which he concluded that the importance of AI applications in education is determined by their ability to suit the needs and abilities of the learners, to work according to their educational preferences, and to monitor the progress rate of each learner. These applications contain tracks that suit all learners, despite differences amongst their levels, boost their learning motivation, and cope with students' low levels of attention [13].

## 7. Conclusion

To conclude, online language learning as well as mobile or web-assisted language learning has become very important learning tools. Most of the renowned language centres have employed online classes together with onsite classes according to the convenience of their learners. This is to save the time and effort wasted in commuting to language centres. As previously mentioned, the Google Bundle is a winner in all online classes as it is the most comprehensive tool that includes whatever is needed for any online class. This is classified under non-traditional language learning classes that involve technology. It is different from the traditional classes, where Learning uses the conventional method of education where learners attend physical classes, the learners interact with the teacher, and follow standardized curriculum material such as textbooks and lectures. It involves face-to-face instruction and teacher-led lessons with limited use of technology.

Web or mobile-assisted language learning applications have become a tool that suits the changes that have come upon our world. A world where everything is rapid and personal time has become very limited due to the busy world we live in. In this busy world, many people have more than one job to be able to satisfy their needs. Family time has become limited to a few minutes due to the struggle for earnings to be able to gain the daily bread. Hence, it has become difficult to join traditional language courses in case one wants to develop oneself and gain a second language. Hence, these types of applications have come as a savior to these people who do not have time. These apps can be used whilst commuting, waiting for a turn, resting at home with the family, or even walking from one place to the other. In other words, they are a very convenient tool for everyone. They are also cheaper than the traditional courses if one subscribe to the Premium or the Pro. Thus, the above tools are considered a qualitative leap in the field of language learning and it is expected that more innovations will follow.

## Author details

Omnia Ibrahim Mohamed[1,2]* and Omar Al-Jadaan[2]

1 Faculty of Languages and Translations, SAMS, Cairo, Egypt

2 RAK Medical and Health Sciences University, United Arab Emirates

*Address all correspondence to: omnia@rakmhsu.ac.ae

## References


[1] Kukulska-Hulme A. Mobile-assisted language learning. In: Chapelle CA, editor. The Encyclopedia of Applied Linguistics. Wiley-Blackwell; 2020. pp. 1-9. DOI: 10.1002/9781405198431.wbeal0768.pub2

[2] Pachler N, Cook J, Bachmair B. Appropriation of mobile cultural resources for learning. International Journal of Mobile and Blended Learning. 2010;**2**(1):1-21

[3] Mohamed OI. The effectiveness of internet and mobile applications in English language learning for health sciences' students in a University in the United Arab Emirates. Arab World English Journal. 2021;**12**(1):181-197. DOI: 10.24093/awej/vol12no1.13

[4] Thornton P, Houser C. Using mobile phones in English education in Japan. Journal of Computer Assisted Learning. 2005;**21**(3):217-228

[5] Loewen S, Crowther D, Isbell D, Kim K, Maloney J, Miller Z, et al. Mobile-assisted language learning: A Duolingo case study. ReCALL. 2019;**31**(3):293-311. DOI: 10.1017/S0958344019000065

[6] Curry D. Babbel Revenue and Usage Statistics. 2023. Available from: www.businessofapps.com/data/babbel-statistics/ [Retrieved from: August 3, 2012]

[7] Sporn Z, Chanter J, Meehan D. Babbel language learning podcasts. International Journal of Advanced Corporate Learning (IJAC). 2020;**13**(3):43-49. DOI: 10.3991/ijac.v13i3.17025S

[8] Mohamed, Lobo. A comparative study between monolingual and bilingual teaching methodologies of English in a Health Sciences University in the United Arab Emirates. English Language Teaching, Canadian Center of Science and Education. 2020;**13**(1):1-73

[9] Detre G, Cooke E, Whately B. Learn a language, memrise is authentic, useful, personalized. 2010. Available from: https://www.memrise.com/ [Accessed: August 1, 2023]

[10] Van V, Anguera X. The world's best way to improve your English pronunciation. 2015. Available from: https://elsaspeak.com/en/ [Accessed: July 29, 2023]

[11] American and British Academy. ABA learn English – Learn English and take it to the next level. 2006. Available from: https://www.abaenglish.com/ [Accessed: July 26, 2023]

[12] Curry D. Babbel revenue and usage statistics. 2023. Available from: www.businessofapps.com/data/language-learning-app-market/ [Retrieved from: August 3, 2012]

[13] Mukhallafi T. Using artificial intelligence for developing English language teaching/learning: An analytical study from university students' perspective. International Journal of English Linguistics. 2020;**10**:40. DOI: 10.5539/ijel.v10n6p40

Chapter 5

# Transforming Medical and Health Sciences Education with Gamification

*Khaled Ouanes*


## Abstract

This chapter explores the burgeoning potential of AI-powered gamification in revolutionizing medical education. Gamification, the application of game design elements in non-game settings, fosters engagement and improves knowledge retention. When infused with AI, gamification offers a personalized learning experience with adaptive difficulty and immersive simulations. This personalized approach empowers both healthcare professionals and patients. The chapter explores the transformative potential of AI-powered gamification for enhancing skill development, knowledge retention, and patient engagement. It also acknowledges the importance of addressing ethical and practical challenges, such as development costs, data privacy, and the potential impact on healthcare culture. By harnessing the strengths of AI and gamification, we can create a future where medical education is not only effective but also engaging and empowering.


**Keywords:** AI-powered gamification, medical education, personalized learning, gamification for medical education, health sciences education

## 1. Introduction

The ever-expanding body of medical knowledge necessitates a continuous evolution in healthcare education. Traditional methods, while valuable, often struggle to keep pace with the need for engaging and interactive learning experiences. This chapter explores the transformative potential of gamification to develop this field. Gamification, defined as "the use of game design elements in non-game contexts" [1], has emerged as a powerful tool in education, particularly within healthcare. By integrating artificial intelligence (AI) with gamification, medical education is undergoing a significant transformation. It is hence very interesting to delve into this exciting synergy, exploring how gamification and AI-powered gamification can create adaptive learning environments that cater to individual learners' needs.

During the last two decades, we have started witnessing the rise of Gamification in Healthcare and medical education. Games have since become a novel pedagogical tool in medical and health sciences education, offering an interactive and engaging learning experience. Research over the past two decades has revealed a burgeoning field with diverse applications. Studies suggest that games can effectively convey complex medical concepts, enhance procedural skills, and foster critical thinking among learners [2]. The integration of gamification elements into educational curricula has further demonstrated the potential to improve knowledge retention, promote behavior change, and facilitate patient education [3]. These findings highlight the promise of gamification and games as a promising avenue for innovation in health sciences education, warranting further exploration and integration into academic programs.

In addition to the fact that gamification offers several advantages over traditional methods for motivating behavior changes toward improved health and well-being [4], and compared to game-based learning and serious games, gamification focuses specifically on incorporating game elements like points, badges, and leaderboards into non-game contexts to enhance education and knowledge acquisition [3, 5]. This distinction allows gamification to be broadly applied within existing educational frameworks.

The integration of AI into gamification solutions marks a transformative movement reshaping medical education and professional development. This innovative intersection of AI and gamification has several implications. Indeed, AI personalizes learning experiences, creates adaptive simulations, and fosters a more engaging environment for students, learners, trainees, healthcare professionals, and patients. Some challenges associated with this emerging field, such as ethical considerations and development costs, still exist.

## 2. The power of gamification

Gamification relies on the application of game-design elements, theories, and principles in non-game settings. By incorporating elements like scores, points, badges, leaderboards, and narrative structures, gamification can deeply transform dry and dense learning material into a more engaging and motivating experience. Studies have shown that gamification, mirroring the captivating nature of games, can lead to improved knowledge retention, increased participation, better student engagement, and enhanced problem-solving skills [6–9].

This approach is particularly pertinent and highly useful in the realm of medical and health sciences education, where the need for interactive, immersive, and practical learning experiences is paramount. The application of gamification in medical education can lead to optimized learning experiences tailored to individual students' needs, weaknesses, learning styles, and even personality traits as evidenced by empirical studies. For instance, the use of a gamified web-based learning environment demonstrated that gamification could affect learners differently based on their personality traits, suggesting a nuanced approach to educational gamification [9].

Within the health sciences and medical education context, gamification elements (points, badges, scores, leaderboards, etc.) can be leveraged to encourage sought-after learning behaviors that promote knowledge acquirement and retention of complex medical information and materials.

Moreover, gamified training platforms, including educational games, mobile medical apps, and virtual patient scenarios, have shown promise in increasing learner engagement and motivation [10]. These platforms allow for the application of real-world scenarios in a risk-free environment, fostering active learning and critical thinking [11]. For instance, Fold It, an online puzzle game based on protein folding, exemplifies how gamification can facilitate complex learning through interactive processes [3].

The advent of technology has further propelled the use of gamified platforms in medical education. Students entering medical schools are technologically literate and expect a diverse educational experience that these platforms can provide [3]. Virtual patient simulations have been effective in enhancing general learning outcomes and are instrumental in teaching clinical reasoning and decision-making skills [12].

The integration of gamification into medical and health sciences education has shown promising results in enhancing learning outcomes and student engagement. Gamification techniques leverage the innate human desire for competition, achievement, and recognition, thereby fostering a more interactive and motivating learning environment. For instance, the use of game-based simulations allows students to practice clinical skills in a risk-free setting, which can lead to improved proficiency and confidence [13].

Additionally, the application of leaderboards, points, and badges in educational platforms can encourage continuous learning and self-improvement among healthcare professionals. It is essential to consider the design and implementation of these gamified elements carefully to ensure they align with educational objectives and enhance the overall learning experience [13].

Gamification strategies in medical education have been applied across various medical disciplines, demonstrating improvements in learning outcomes and clinical decision-making abilities [10].

Despite the potential benefits, the field faces challenges in conducting rigorous research to evaluate the efficacy of gamified learning tools. There is a need for well-designed studies and research to confirm the advantages of these educational interventions. As the body of scientific literature grows, it is anticipated that gamification will become an integral component of medical education, offering a dynamic and interactive learning environment that aligns with the needs of modern learners [3].

While gamification has shown promise in medical education, challenges such as ensuring the relevance and effectiveness of games, as well as integrating them into the curriculum, remain. As previously established, future research should focus on the long-term impact of gamification on medical education and its potential to transform traditional learning environments [14].

Gamification represents a paradigm shift in medical education, offering immersive and engaging learning experiences6. Their potential to revolutionize medical education warrants further exploration and integration into educational strategies [14].

## 3. AI and gamification: a perfect match

Artificial intelligence (AI) brings a new dimension to gamification in medical and healthcare education. Indeed, the effectiveness of gamification in medical education can be augmented and clearly enhanced by AI technologies and techniques that adapt the learning environment to the individual's learning style and pace. AI algorithms can examine and analyze students' interactions with the gamified elements, understand their level and style of learning, and consequently adjust the difficulty level of the tasks or suggest different learning paths, thus providing a personalized and optimally customized learning experience.

To ensure the successful implementation of AI-powered gamification educational solutions and systems, it is also crucial to consider the diverse impacts of gamification elements on different personality traits. For example, introverted students may respond more positively to badges, while extroverted students may be more motivated by scores, points, and leaderboards [15]. Such insights underscore the importance of personalizing gamification strategies to cater to the varied preferences and traits of medical students and learners.

As previously stated, AI algorithms can personalize learning experiences by tailoring content and difficulty to individual needs. AI algorithms will learn to better customize and tweak the learning materials for each individual learner with every interaction that occurs with them. Imagine a medical student using an AI-powered gamification learning platform that adapts to their strengths, weaknesses, learning pace, learning style, and personality traits, presenting targeted challenges and feedback in a simulated environment. Thanks to AI, these environments and learning experiences will keep improving and becoming more and more adapted to this individual learner.

Hence, we can highlight that the integration of AI algorithms and techniques in gamified learning platforms has marked a transformative and innovative step in medical and healthcare education. These novel approaches of utilizing AI techniques, alongside Natural Language Processing (NLP) tools, have been shown to optimize the effectiveness of learning by personalizing the experience to each user [16]. This individualized learning is crucial in disseminating knowledge about low-value medical practices—procedures where the potential risk clearly outweighs the benefits—which are a significant concern for healthcare quality and sustainability [17, 18].

Reconfigurable and personalized gamification platforms, as proposed by Fernández et al. [16], leverage the engaging elements of gamification, such as scoring systems, challenges, leaderboards, and rewards, within a non-gaming context to enhance student engagement. The platform's adaptability, powered by AI, allows for the adjustment of question difficulty and types, as well as the level of gamification, to suit individual preferences, thereby improving learning outcomes [16]. Such platforms will enhance the adaptive and precision learning experience for all learners regardless of their individual attributes and level of knowledge.

Moreover, the collaborative aspect of these platforms fosters a collective, community-driven approach to learning. Students participate in projects such as creating a specialized dictionary for do-not-do terms, which not only enhances engagement but also contributes to the development of an automatic translation system through NLP and transformers [16]. This system becomes an additional learning resource, evolving and partially self-improving and self-maintaining over time. This is a very important aspect as enhancing the collaborative and teamwork skills of medical and health sciences students and learners is paramount, considering that they will operate in highly cooperative, teamwork-driven settings within healthcare organizations.

The implications of such AI-powered gamification in healthcare education systems are profound. By aiming to reduce the prevalence of low-value practices, we can fulfill an obvious potential for significant improvements in patient safety and reductions in healthcare costs [19, 20]. The adaptability, flexibility, and collaborative nature of these platforms promise to make continuous education in healthcare more effective, efficient, and engaging, paving the way for a future where medical professionals are better equipped to provide high-quality care. This is vital in the overall context of expanding medical knowledge.

As previously discussed, the application of AI in gamified learning experiences within health sciences and medical education allows for the personalization of learning paths and paces, consequently providing feedback and challenges tailored to the learner's actual progress. This approach aligns with the theory of gamified learning, which posits that instructional content influences learning outcomes and learners' behaviors [21]. Moreover, the motivational effect of game elements can be enhanced and customized with AI. As already demonstrated, this motivational effect can be explained by various theories, including the self-determination theory, which defines three universal psychological basic needs: competence, autonomy, and social inclusion [22]. When these needs are addressed through gamification elements, positive effects on behavior and its determinants are observed. Indeed, self-determination theory stipulates that the satisfaction of psychological needs for competence, autonomy, and social relatedness is central to intrinsic motivation and high-quality learning [23], which AI-powered gamification can effectively facilitate.

AI techniques are also used to recognize individual student difficulties and provide targeted content based on student performance, enhancing personalized learning experiences [24]. Besides, some AI-based gamification services in education can examine and analyze predicted learning attitudes and behaviors to increase learning efficiency and provide superior immersive experiences [25].

In such context, gamification supported by AI, can lead to the development of critical skills, including soft skills, through simulation and interactive scenarios. For instance, gamified simulations that incorporate AI can mimic patient interactions, organizational workflows, and medical procedures, offering a safe and controlled environment for students, learners, and trainees to practice and hone their skills in an individualized manner. Such applications have been shown to yield positive results, with studies indicating that gamification can improve technical skills and competences in healthcare settings. Adaptive gamification in e-learning utilizes AI to tailor gamification mechanics and dynamics to the personality, needs, values, and motivations of each learner, creating an intelligent adaptive learning environment [26].

At present, the use of gamification in medical and healthcare education is a growing area of interest, with several opportunities that have the potential to enhance learning experiences and improve student engagement on different sides and levels [27]. The integration of other AI elements, particularly large language models (LLMs) like ChatGPT, has the potential to further improve medical education by providing students with detailed information and interactive simulations [28]. ChatGPT, and other LLMs, can also be used to enhance clinical management processes and provide support and treatment recommendations [29]. Machine learning (ML) techniques, on the other hand, are crucial in educating the next generation of medical professionals, enabling them to become part of the emerging data science revolution [30].

Artificial Intelligence (AI) techniques, including Machine Learning (ML) and Deep Learning (DL), are increasingly being integrated into medical education. These technologies offer innovative approaches to training medical students and professionals, enhancing their learning experience through gamification and other interactive methods.

AI-powered gamification holds significant potential for drastically transforming medical and health sciences education. By harnessing the power of AI to tailor gamification elements to individual learners, educators can create engaging, effective, and personalized learning experiences that prepare students for the challenges of the healthcare industry.

## 4. Revolutionizing learning with AI-powered gamification: applications and benefits

AI takes gamification in medical education to a whole new level. By analyzing learner performance and progress, AI tailors personalized learning paths. This ensures students focus on areas needing improvement, maximizing their learning experience. AI can even go beyond static simulations by creating adaptive simulations. Imagine a virtual patient scenario that responds to a learner's decisions in real-time, fostering crucial clinical reasoning and decision-making skills in a safe, controlled environment [9, 24].

Gamification, especially when it is AI-based, is not just for students. Complex medical situations can be presented as interactive case studies. AI can award points and/or badges for accurate diagnoses and treatment choices, fostering a spirit of healthy competition and knowledge sharing through leaderboards. This creates a dynamic learning experience that goes beyond rote memorization.

The benefits extend beyond medical professionals and students. Patients can leverage AI-powered chatbots that deliver personalized health information and education in an engaging format. Gamified elements within these chatbots can encourage patients to adhere to treatment plans and actively participate in preventative care, empowering them to take charge of their well-being.

The power of AI-powered gamification lies in its ability to enhance learning experiences and improve knowledge retention. Gamification techniques and strategies increase learner motivation and engagement, leading to a deeper, long-lasting understanding of complex medical concepts.

Enhanced skill development is another key benefit. AI-powered simulations provide learners with opportunities to practice complex medical skills in a safe and repeatable manner. This allows for experimentation and refinement without the risk of real-world consequences. Perhaps the most significant advantage is the ability to personalize learning. AI caters to individual learning styles and paces, ensuring every learner progresses at their optimal rate. This fosters a sense of agency and control over the learning process [31, 32].

The impact is not limited to medical students and professionals. Gamified patient education tools powered by AI can increase patient engagement, empowering them to take an active role in their health and well-being. This collaborative approach can lead to better health outcomes overall.

By leveraging research insights, AI takes gamification for health and medical sciences education several steps further. Studies have shown the effectiveness of AI in delivering personalized content, and tailoring educational materials to address specific student needs. Additionally, adaptive learning platforms powered by AI techniques like Natural Language Processing (NLP) further enhance engagement by adapting the gamification experience to each individual user. This ensures the learning experience remains relevant and stimulating [16].

AI-enhanced gamification platforms hold immense potential for continuous education and quality care. These platforms can be designed to continuously educate healthcare professionals about low-value practices, keeping them updated with the latest recommendations. This ultimately translates to improved healthcare quality and better patient outcomes.

## 5. Challenges and considerations

Despite the potential benefits, the current body of evidence involving the combination of game-based methods and AI in health is limited. Most studies focus on rehabilitation, particularly motion impairment, and cognitive impairment rather than the implementation of gamification for educational reasons [33]. More research is needed to explore the effectiveness of AI-powered gamification across the wider spectrum of medical education and patient care.

Looking ahead, the field is likely to embrace adaptive game design. AI will assess learners' skill levels and adjust difficulty dynamically, creating a feedback loop that personalizes the learning experience. This approach has the potential to seamlessly integrate with traditional therapy sessions, boosting motivation and engagement for students [34].

Innovative technology, especially when based on AI techniques, is expensive. A growing body of research establishes the high costs associated with implementing novel AI algorithms and systems, including data acquisition and quality issues [35]. Development costs present another significant challenge. Creating sophisticated AI-powered gamification platforms, systems, solutions, and applications requires substantially significant investment [36].

Finding sustainable funding models will be crucial for widespread adoption. Indeed, several publications emphasize this need for sustainable funding models for AI projects in general, particularly in the context of sustainable finances [37, 38].

Data privacy and security are paramount concerns in the context of any e-health systems or solutions. Similarly, when developing gamification platforms and applications, we need to ensure the cybersecurity and the privacy of the data and the different end-users. Robust measures must be implemented to ensure patient information remains confidential and protected ([39]: [40]).

Finally, the potential impact of gamification on healthcare culture warrants consideration. While healthy competition can be motivating, it is crucial to ensure gamification fosters collaboration, not a culture of rivalry, within healthcare settings. In the vast realm of medical and healthcare education, the ethical considerations of gamification – for education and for other usages – are paramount. As Shahri et al. [41] elucidate, gamification can straddle the line between a motivational tool and a source of unjustified and undue pressure, potentially impacting social and mental well-being in educational institutions or within healthcare organizations, leading to unwanted tensions and conflicts. Ethical deployment in healthcare education necessitates a balance, ensuring gamification does not devolve into "exploitation-ware" [42], where the drive for virtual rewards overtakes or, at least, overshadows the intrinsic value of learning and patient care. We need to standardize an ethical framework that must be sensitive to personal and cultural values, safeguard privacy, and foster an environment where gamification serves as an enhancement rather than a detriment to the educational experience [43]. Thus, when integrating gamification into medical curricula, educators should heed clear ethical guidelines to maintain the integrity and efficacy of the learning process.

By addressing these challenges and continuing research, AI-powered educational gamification for health and medical sciences can unlock its full potential to pursue its groundbreaking impact on medical education and patient care.

## 6. Conclusion

This chapter has explored the exciting potential of gamification, particularly AI-powered gamification, in revolutionizing medical education. Gamification, defined as "the use of game design elements in non-game contexts" [1], offers a compelling alternative to traditional teaching methods [14]. By incorporating game elements like points, badges, and leaderboards, and by harnessing the power of AI techniques, gamified learning environments foster engagement, improve knowledge retention, and enhance problem-solving skills [9].

The integration of AI into gamification marks a transformative leap forward. AI personalizes learning experiences by tailoring content and difficulty to individual needs [16]. This personalization caters to diverse learning styles and paces, ensuring optimal learning outcomes [15]. Furthermore, AI-powered simulations create immersive and realistic scenarios, allowing learners to practice critical skills in a safe, controlled environment [25]. These simulations foster clinical reasoning and decision-making abilities, ultimately improving preparedness for real-world situations [13].

The benefits extend beyond medical students and professionals. Gamified patient education tools powered by AI can empower patients to take an active role in their health and well-being [3]. Interactive case studies and AI-powered chatbots that deliver personalized health information can increase patient engagement and adherence to treatment plans [29]. This collaborative approach between patients and healthcare providers can lead to better health outcomes overall.

However, realizing the full potential of this exciting field necessitates careful consideration of ethical and practical challenges. Development costs for sophisticated AI-powered games can be significant, requiring innovative funding models for widespread adoption [34]. Additionally, ensuring data privacy and security is paramount when developing healthcare gamification applications [24]. Finally, the potential impact of gamification on healthcare culture requires close examination. Gamification should foster collaboration within healthcare settings, not a culture of competition [26].

Additionally, we have to recognize that AI-powered gamification ushers in a transformative era for medical education. It leverages the power of AI to personalize learning journeys, craft immersive simulations, and boost learner motivation. This innovative approach has the potential to revolutionize education, not just by improving knowledge retention and enhancing skill development, but also by empowering both healthcare professionals and patients. As with any groundbreaking advancements, careful consideration of ethical and practical challenges is paramount to unlocking the full potential of this exciting field. While the integration of AI in games is not a novel concept, its capabilities have the power to significantly alter classroom dynamics, paving the way for a more engaging and effective learning experience [36].

This chapter provides a springboard for further research into AI-powered gamification for medical and health sciences education. Some potential areas of exploration:

- The long-term impact of AI-powered gamification on healthcare professional competency.
- The development of cost-effective AI solutions for healthcare gamification.
- The integration of gamification with other educational technologies like extended reality (XR) and/or virtual reality (VR).
- The development of better AI-based systems capable of autonomously evolving and adapting throughout the academic journey of the learners.
- The development of better security, privacy, and ethics guidelines and frameworks.

Gamification appears to be at least as effective as traditional learning for improving knowledge, skills, and satisfaction in health professions education, but more rigorous research is needed [44].

Indeed, it is obvious that the potential benefits of gamification, especially when based on AI, for improving knowledge retention, skill development, and learner engagement are promising. However, the long-term impact on healthcare professional competency necessitates further investigation. Longitudinal studies are crucial to assess certain facets such as:

- *Transfer of learning to real-world practice*: Do the skills honed through gamified simulations translate effectively to real-world clinical settings? Research designs could involve observing healthcare professionals who have utilized AI-powered gamification in their training and comparing their performance with those who have not. Standardized clinical assessments and patient outcomes could be used as evaluation metrics.

- *Retention of knowledge and skills over time*: Does the gamified learning experience lead to long-term sustained knowledge and skills retention among healthcare students and professionals? Longitudinal studies with regular knowledge and skills assessments at predetermined intervals (e.g., 6 months, 1 year, 3 years) could provide valuable insights and guidance.

- *Impact on clinical decision-making*: Does AI-powered gamification enhance clinical decision-making abilities and skills? Studies could involve comparing the decision-making accuracy of healthcare professionals who have undergone gamified training, or a combination of gamified and conventional training, with those who have not, using simulated scenarios mirroring real-world situations and settings.

### 6.1 Methodologies for research

- *Randomized controlled trials (RCTs)*: These studies would involve randomly assigning healthcare professionals to either an AI-powered gamified learning group or a control group receiving traditional training. Long-term patient outcomes and clinical performance could then be compared between the groups. Such studies should be conducted over a reasonably long period of time.

- *Cohort studies*: These studies would follow a group of healthcare professionals who have undergone AI-powered gamified training and/or education over an extended period, tracking their knowledge retention, skill development, and impact on patient care quality.

- *Mixed-methods research*: This approach would combine quantitative data (e.g., test scores, patients' health outcomes) with qualitative data (e.g., surveys, interviews, focus groups) to gain a more comprehensive and holistic understanding of the long-term impact of AI-powered gamification on healthcare professionals.

Through implementing these research directions and methodologies, we can gain valuable insights into the long-term effectiveness of AI-powered gamification in medical education. This will ultimately inform the development of even more impactful educational tools and strategies for healthcare professionals. By continuing to explore and develop AI-powered healthcare gamification, we can create a future where learning is not just effective, but also engaging and empowering for all.

## Author details

Khaled Ouanes
Department of Health Informatics, College of Health Sciences, Saudi Electronic University, Dammam, Saudi Arabia

*Address all correspondence to: k.ouanes@seu.edu.sa

## References

[1] Deterding S, Dixon D, Khaled R, Nacke L. From game design elements to gamefulness: Defining gamification. In: Proceedings of the 15th International Academic MindTrek Conference: Envisioning Future Media Environments. Tampere, Finland; 2011. pp. 9-15

[2] Kharrazi H, Lu AS, Gharghabi F, Coleman W. A scoping review of health game research: Past, present, and future. Games for Health Journal. 2012;**1**(2): 153-164. DOI: 10.1089/g4h.2012.0011

[3] Krishnamurthy K, Selvaraj N, Gupta P, Cyriac B, Dhurairaj P, Abdullah A, et al. Benefits of gamification in medical education. Clinical Anatomy. 2022;**35**:795-807. DOI: 10.1002/ca.23916

[4] Johnson D, Deterding S, Kuhn K, Staneva A, Stoyanov S, Hides L. Gamification for health and wellbeing: A systematic review of the literature. Internet Interventions. 2016;**6**:89-106. DOI: 10.1016/j.invent.2016.10.002

[5] Gorbanev I, Agudelo-Londoño S, González RA, Cortes A, Pomares A, Delgadillo V, et al. A systematic review of serious games in medical education: Quality of evidence and pedagogical strategy. Medical Education Online. 2018;**23**(1):1438718

[6] Dichev C, Dicheva D. Gamifying education: What is known, what is believed and what remains uncertain: A critical review. International Journal of Educational Technology in Higher Education. 2017;**14**:9. DOI: 10.1186/s41239-017-0042-5

[7] Jang J, Park JJY, Yi MY. Gamification of online learning. In: Conati C, Heffernan N, Mitrovic A, Verdejo MF, editors. In Artificial Intelligence in Education. Cham: Springer; 2015. pp. 646-649

[8] Sailer M, Homner L. The gamification of learning: A meta-analysis. Educational Psychology Review. 2020;**32**:77-112. DOI: 10.1007/s10648-019-09498-w

[9] Smiderle R, Rigo SJ, Marques LB, et al. The impact of gamification on students' learning, engagement and behavior based on their personality traits. Smart Learning Environments. 2020;**7**:3. DOI: 10.1186/s40561-019-0098-x

[10] McCoy L, Lewis JH, Dalton D. Gamification and multimedia for medical education: A landscape review. The Journal of the American Osteopathic Association. 2016;**116**(1):22-34. DOI: 10.7556/jaoa.2016.003

[11] Bochennek K, Wittekindt B, Zimmermann S-Y, Klingebiel T. More than mere games: A review of card and board games for medical education. Medical Teacher. 2007;**29**(9-10):941-948. DOI: 10.1080/01421590701749813

[12] Kononowicz AA, Woodham LA, Edelbring S, Stathakarou N, Davies D, Saxena N, et al. Virtual patient simulations in health professions education: Systematic review and meta-analysis by the digital health education collaboration. Journal of Medical Internet Research. 2019;**21**(7):e14676. DOI: 10.2196/14676

[13] Salehi A, Mohammadi H, Jenabi E, Khanlarzadeh E, Ashtari K. Quality of evidence and pedagogical strategy in using gamification in medical education literature: A systematic review. Simulation and Gaming. 2023;**54**:598-620. DOI: 10.1177/10468781231195903

[14] Xu M, Luo Y, Zhang Y, Xia R, Qian H, Zou X. Game-based learning in medical education. Frontiers in Public Health. 2023. DOI: 10.3389/fpubh.2023.1113682

[15] Jia Y, Xu B, Karanam Y, Voida S. Personality-targeted gamification: A survey study on personality traits and motivational affordances. In: Proceedings of the 2016 CHI Conference on Human Factors in Computing Systems-CHI '16. San Jose, California, USA; 2016. DOI: 10.1145/2858036.2858515 ACM

[16] Fernández C, Vicente M, Lorenzo S, Carrillo I, Guilabert M. Reconfigurable gamification platform for the autonomous learning of low value medical practices. Signal and Image Processing Trends. 2022. DOI: 10.5121/csit.2022.121716

[17] Chassin MR, Galvin RW. The urgent need to improve health care quality. JAMA. 1998;**280**:1000-1058

[18] Korenstein D, Chimonas S. Reducing overuse-is patient safety the answer? JAMA. 2017;**317**:810-110

[19] Brownlee S, Chalkidou K, Doust J, et al. Evidence for overuse of medical services around the world. Lancet. 2017;**390**:157-686

[20] Shrank WH, Rogstad TL, Parekh N. Waste in the US health care system: Estimated costs and potential for savings 11. Journal of the American Medical Association. 2019. DOI: 10.1001/jama.2019.13978

[21] Landers RN. Developing a theory of gamified learning: Linking serious games and gamification of learning. Simulation and Gaming. 2014;**45**(6):752-768

[22] Sailer M, Hense JU, Mayr SK, Mandl H. How gamification motivates: An experimental study of the effects of specific game design elements on psychological need satisfaction. Computers in Human Behavior. 2017;**69**:371-380. DOI: 10.1016/j.chb.2016.12.033

[23] Ryan RM, Deci EL. Overview of self-determination theory: An organismic dialectical perspective. In: Deci EL, Ryan RM, editors. Handbook of Self-determination Research. Rochester, NY, US: University of Rochester Press; 2002. pp. 3-33

[24] Bracaccio R, Hojaij F, Notargiacomo P. Gamification in the study of anatomy: The use of artificial intelligence to improve learning. The FASEB Journal. 2019;**33**. DOI: 10.1096/fasebj.2019.33.1_supplement.444.28

[25] Nam H. Design of AI-based gamification platform for effective educational service using child behavior prediction/change. Turkish Journal of Computer and Mathematics Education (TURCOMAT). 2021;**12**:286-292. DOI: 10.17762/TURCOMAT.V12I5.899

[26] Bennani S, Maalel A, Ghézala H. Adaptive gamification in E-learning: A literature review and future challenges. Computer Applications in Engineering Education. 2021;**30**:628-642. DOI: 10.1002/cae.22477

[27] Nicola S, Virag I, Stoicu-Tivadar L. VR medical gamification for training and education. Studies in Health Technology and Informatics. 2017;**236**:97-103

[28] Lee H. The rise of Chat GPT: Exploring its potential in medical education. Anatomical Sciences Education. 2023;**00**:1-6. DOI: 10.1002/ase.2270

[29] Tariq S, Tariq S. Revolutionizing healthcare with AI: The role of chat GPT. Journal of University Medical and Dental

College. 2023;**14**(2):v-v. DOI: 10.37723/jumdc.v14i2.850

[30] Kolachalama VB, Garg PS. Machine learning and medical education. npj Digital Medicine. 2018;**1**:54. DOI: 10.1038/s41746-018-0061-1

[31] Maghsudi S, Lan A, Xu J, van der Schaar M. Personalized Education in the Artificial Intelligence Era: What to Expect Next. IEEE Signal Processing Magazine. 2021;**38**(3):37-50. DOI: 10.1109/MSP.2021.3055032

[32] UNESCO. Understanding the Impact of Artificial Intelligence on Skills Development. United Nations Educational, Scientific and Cultural Organization; 2021. Available from: https://unevoc.unesco.org/pub/understanding_the_impact_of_ai_on_skills_development.pdf

[33] Tolks D, Schmidt JJ, Kuhn S. The role of Ai in serious games and gamification for health: Scoping review. JMIR Serious Games. 2024;**12**:e48258. DOI: 10.2196/48258

[34] Burdea G, Kim N, Polistico K, Kadaru A, Grampurohit N, Roll D, et al. Assistive game controller for artificial intelligence-enhanced telerehabilitation post-stroke. Assistive Technology. 2021;**33**(3):117-128. DOI: 10.1080/10400435.2019.1593260 Available from: https://europepmc.org/abstract/MED/31180276

[35] Kejriwal M. AI in practice and implementation: Issues and costs. In: Artificial Intelligence for Industries of the Future. Future of Business and Finance. In, Cham: Springer; 2023. DOI: 10.1007/978-3-031-19039-1_2

[36] Kurni M, Mohammed MS, Srinivasa KG. AI-enabled gamification in education. In: A Beginner's Guide to Introduce Artificial Intelligence in Teaching and Learning. Cham: Springer; 2023. DOI: 10.1007/978-3-031-32653-0_6

[37] Musleh Al-Sartawi AMA, Hussainey K, Razzaque A. The role of artificial intelligence in sustainable finance. Journal of Sustainable Finance and Investment. 2022:1-6. DOI: 10.1080/20430795.2022.2057405

[38] Pashang, S., Weber, O. (2023). AI for sustainable finance: Governance mechanisms for institutional and societal approaches. In: Mazzi, F., Floridi, L. (eds) The Ethics of Artificial Intelligence for the Sustainable Development Goals. Philosophical Studies Series, vol 152. Springer, Cham. doi:10.1007/978-3-031-21147-8_12

[39] Mavroeidi A-G, Kitsiou A, Kalloniatis C. The Role of Gamification in Privacy Protection and User Engagement. London, UK: IntechOpen; 2020. DOI: 10.5772/intechopen.91159

[40] Shojaei P, Vlahu-Gjorgievska E, Chow Y-W. Security and privacy of technologies in health information systems: A systematic literature review. Computers. 2024;**13**(2):41. DOI: 10.3390/computers13020041

[41] Shahri A, Hosseini M, Phalp K, Taylor J, Ali R. Towards a code of ethics for gamification at enterprise. In: Frank U, Loucopoulos P, Pastor Ó, Petrounias I, editors. The Practice of Enterprise Modeling. Vol. 197. Berlin, Heidelberg: Springer; 2014. pp. 235-245

[42] Nicholson S.A User-Centered Theoretical Framework for Meaningful Gamification A Brief. Games+ Learning+ Society 8. 2012

[43] Friedman B et al. Value sensitive design and information systems. In: Early Engagement and New technologies:

Opening up the laboratory. Vol. 2. Netherlands: Springer; 2013. p. 55, 95

[44] Gentry S, Gauthier A, Ehrstrom B, Wortley D, Lilienthal A, Car L, et al. Serious gaming and gamification education in health professions: Systematic review. Journal of Medical Internet Research. 2019:21. DOI: 10.2196/12994

Chapter 6

# Unveiling the Holistic Approach of the STEAME Teacher Facilitators Academy Project

*Paula Escudeiro, Márcia Campos Gouveia, Nuno Escudeiro and Francisca Escudeiro*


## Abstract

The field of education is increasingly recognizing the importance of fostering students' abilities through project-based learning across disciplines. To address the challenges faced by teachers, especially in Science, Technology, Engineering, Arts, Mathematics, and Entrepreneurship (STEAME) fields, the STEAME Teacher Facilitators Academy project is dedicated to comprehensive training and support. It aims to develop a Teacher Facilitators Competence Framework, guiding teacher education providers in integrating STEAME teaching into programs. The project will offer accessible learning modules and workshops for both students and teachers, fostering competence in STEAME teaching. Collaboration among teachers will be promoted through a community of practice and mentoring program. The ultimate goal is to guide teachers toward Education 3.0 and 4.0, leveraging the latest trends and technologies for a world-class education. The project's pioneering solutions have the potential to influence teacher development and elevate education quality in Europe, creating a transformative educational landscape through local academies.


**Keywords:** project-based learning, STEAME education, teacher training, educational innovation, local academies

## 1. Introduction

In the dynamic landscape of modern education, the imperative to equip students with essential competencies and skills for their future success has never been more pressing. At the forefront of this endeavor is the growing recognition of the transformative potential inherent in multidisciplinary, project-based learning methodologies. These approaches, driven by a vision to cultivate the innovators and problem-solvers of tomorrow, underscore the pivotal roles played by educators and aspiring teachers in shaping the educational landscape.

At the forefront of this transformative journey lies the Science, Technology, Engineering, Arts, Mathematics, and Entrepreneurship (STEAME) Teacher Facilitators Academy—an ambitious initiative poised to revolutionize educational landscapes into dynamic hubs of Science, Technology, Engineering, Arts,

Mathematics, and Entrepreneurship (STEAME) project-based learning. Anchored in the profound belief in the transformative power of education, this initiative places teacher facilitators at its core, recognizing their indispensable role in nurturing competencies and skills among students.

This chapter explores the conceptual framework of the STEAME Teacher Facilitators Academy, illuminating its mission to catalyze the metamorphosis of educational institutions into vibrant STEAME learning ecosystems. Through a meticulous examination of its pioneering innovations, overarching objectives, and targeted solutions, it aims to unravel the tapestry of this transformative endeavor.

In light of mounting evidence highlighting the challenges faced by educators, particularly in STEAME fields, the STEAME Teacher Facilitators Academy endeavors to bridge critical gaps in teacher competence, tools, and methodologies. By providing comprehensive training and support mechanisms, this initiative aspires to empower educators with the requisite skills to orchestrate impactful project-based learning experiences.

Central to the ethos of the STEAME Teacher Facilitators Academy is its commitment to delivering holistic solutions that address the multifaceted challenges identified by leading educational organizations such as the Organisation for Economic Co-operation and Development (OECD). Through the prism of a comprehensive Teacher Facilitators Competence Framework, this initiative endeavors to chart a path toward educational excellence, ensuring alignment between curriculum intent and learning outcomes.

Moreover, the STEAME Teacher Facilitators Academy champions the ethos of collaboration and networking among educators. By fostering a robust community of practice and mentorship program, this initiative aims to cultivate a culture of continuous improvement, propelling educators toward the vanguard of educational innovation.

With its visionary approach, innovative solutions, and unwavering commitment to excellence, the STEAME Teacher Facilitators Academy stands poised to redefine the contours of teacher development and educational quality across Europe. Through collaborative endeavors and a steadfast dedication to empowering educators, this initiative heralds a new era of educational excellence, where students are inspired to embrace learning as a transformative journey toward a brighter tomorrow.

## 2. Understanding the educational landscape: a review of current trends

Science, technology, engineering and mathematics (STEM) and STEAM education have attracted considerable interest in recent years, given their pivotal role in equipping students for contemporary workforce demands and stimulating innovation. Understanding the present terrain, hurdles, prospects, and developments in STEM and STEAM education necessitates a thorough literature review. This section delves into a curated collection of pivotal references encompassing diverse facets of STEM and STEAM education, spanning from theoretical frameworks to pragmatic methodologies and empirical research discoveries.

As an introduction to STEM education, in Song et al. [1], the authors provide an overview of STEM teacher education within the context of reforms in science teacher education programs for the STEM era, while in Thomas and Huffman [2], the authors discuss the challenges and opportunities associated with the transition from STEM to STEAM education, emphasizing the integration of arts into traditional STEM disciplines.

Moving on to the advancements and innovations in STEM education, Anderson and Li [3] conducts a comprehensive global analysis of STEM education, highlighting the critical importance of integrated approaches. Through international examples, Anderson underscores the necessity of cohesive STEM education in preparing students for modern challenges. This work serves as a valuable resource for educators and policymakers aiming to foster effective STEM education practices. In Ryoo and Winkelmann [4], the authors present a book on innovative learning environments in higher education STEM disciplines, exploring opportunities, challenges, and future directions in the field, and Williams [5] introduces the necessity for change in academic settings, particularly in STEM education. It highlights the common scenarios where change becomes imperative, such as outdated teaching methods, ineffective department policies, or the need for institutional vibrancy. It emphasizes the limitations of change theory alone and the importance of practical guidance based on research. The book aims to provide actionable tools and support for individuals seeking to initiate or navigate changes in STEM education, fostering a community of change-makers committed to improving their respective campuses.

When it comes to teacher education and professional development in STEM, the author in Burrows et al. [6] delves into the critical intersection of teacher professional development and integrated STEM education. Highlighting the importance of dedicated time for practical implementation within the integrated STEM framework, this book offers insights into effective strategies for teacher learning and development. It serves as a valuable resource for educators, curriculum developers, and policymakers, emphasizing the significance of hands-on experiences in fostering effective integrated STEM education.

In Al-Balushi et al. [7], the book *Reforming Science Teacher Education Programs in the STEM Era* examines international and comparative perspectives on reforming science teacher education programs within the STEM era.

The author in Geesa et al. [8] underscores the critical need for integrative STEM education in response to rapid global changes and the widening gap between societal demands and educational responses. It advocates for merging STEM with other disciplines to nurture creative problem-solvers in a technology-driven society. School leaders play a pivotal role in driving this shift, and the book offers insights, strategies, and resources for them. Drawing on research and experiences from successful STEM programs, it provides a comprehensive guide for educational leaders striving to develop, implement, and sustain integrative STEM initiatives in schools and districts.

In terms of interdisciplinary approaches and perspectives in STEM education, Fomunyam [9] delves into theoretical frameworks and concepts related to STEM education, providing insights into the theoretical underpinnings of the field.

In Khine and Areepattamannil [10], the authors explore the theory and practice of STEAM education, covering curriculum design, pedagogical approaches, and implementation strategies integrating arts into STEM, detailing the shift toward interdisciplinary education in the twenty-first century. Acknowledging the need for skills beyond traditional subjects, the book advocates for integrating arts alongside Science, Technology, Engineering, and Mathematics disciplines. It highlights the importance of creativity, innovation, and entrepreneurship in preparing students for future challenges. Chapters delve into practical applications, such as inquiry-based learning, problem-solving investigations, and design thinking, offering strategies for educators to implement STEAM initiatives effectively. Overall, the review underscores STEAM's role in fostering holistic learning and preparing students for diverse career paths in an evolving global landscape.

Addressing contemporary issues and future directions in STEM education, in Kaya-Capocci and Peters-Burton [11] the author brings together diverse perspectives on the convergence of STEM education and entrepreneurial mindsets. Exploring innovative approaches, the book integrates science, technology, engineering, and mathematics with an entrepreneurial focus. Contributors delve into practical strategies and case studies, offering valuable insights into cultivating entrepreneurial thinking within STEM learning environments. This comprehensive resource caters to educators and policymakers seeking to instill an entrepreneurial mindset in STEM education, providing actionable guidance for implementation.

In Delahunty and Ní Ríordáin [12], the authors discuss perspectives in contemporary STEM education research, offering an insightful overview of current research trends in STEM education by examining various perspectives, methodologies, and findings. It serves as a crucial resource for scholars, educators, and policymakers interested in staying abreast of the latest developments in STEM education research.

Drawing from the study conducted by the Johnson et al. [13], this handbook offers an extensive exploration of research in STEM education, encompassing a wide range of topics. It provides insights into current trends, methodologies, and findings, bringing together diverse perspectives from leading experts. Serving as an invaluable reference, it is essential for educators, researchers, and policymakers seeking to advance STEM education practices and stay abreast of the latest developments in the field.

In Wilson-Kennedy et al. [14], the authors explore methods, practices, and programs aimed at broadening participation in STEM, particularly focusing on effective strategies to increase diversity in higher education STEM fields. It compiles effective methods, practices, and programs aimed at fostering inclusivity within STEM education and professions. Contributors share experiences and explore successful strategies to engage underrepresented groups, break down barriers, and promote diversity in STEM. This invaluable resource caters to educators, policymakers, and practitioners seeking insights into creating more inclusive and equitable STEM environments.

Exploring emerging trends and technologies in STEM education, in Allan et al. [15] the author explores innovative approaches to education at the intersection of science, technology, engineering, and mathematics, particularly focusing on blended learning in higher education settings. Allan examines how integrating digital and traditional learning methods can enhance STEM education. With practical examples and research findings, this work provides valuable guidance for educators aiming to implement blended learning strategies in STEM higher education contexts, contributing to ongoing discussions on optimizing teaching methodologies.

According to the findings of the study by the author in Schuck et al. [16], there is a complex landscape of teacher education, focusing on scenarios, political influences, and the role of STEM education. Through insightful analyses, the authors navigate challenges and potential disruptions in teacher education, offering a nuanced understanding of the forces shaping its future. This book is essential for anyone interested in the future of teacher education and the role of STEM therein.

In Barak and Yuan [17], the author sheds light on the intersection of cultural perspectives, project-based learning, and innovative thinking development. By exploring how cultural factors influence educational practices, particularly within project-based learning contexts, researchers provide insights into cultivating innovative thinking skills. This work is valuable for educators and researchers seeking to understand the cultural dimensions of fostering innovation through project-based learning approaches.

Finally, in Demir and Önal [18], the author investigates the impact of technology-assisted and project-based learning approaches on students' attitudes toward mathematics and academic achievement. Examining instructional approaches and student outcomes, the study offers insights into integrating technology and project-based methods in mathematics education. It provides valuable insights into how technology and project-based learning can affect students' attitudes toward mathematics and academic performance.

In conclusion, the selected references offer a multifaceted view of STEM and STEAM education, encompassing theoretical insights, practical strategies, and empirical research findings. They underscore the importance of interdisciplinary approaches, experiential learning, and inclusive practices in fostering student engagement and success in STEM and STEAM disciplines. As educators, policymakers, and researchers navigate the evolving landscape of STEM education, these resources serve as valuable guides for informed decision-making and innovative practices in the field.

## 3. The STEAME Teacher Facilitators Academy

The STEAME Academy emerges as a groundbreaking initiative poised to redefine the educational landscape of Europe through innovation and purpose-driven strategies. At its core lies a meticulously crafted methodology designed to propel European education toward excellence, innovation, and collaboration.

With a keen focus on integrating STEAME principles, the academy endeavors not only to equip educators with essential skills but also to catalyze a transformative shift in the quality and effectiveness of education across the region.

This introductory section delves into the foundational concepts and overarching mission of the STEAME Academy, shedding light on its strategic approach to leveraging the latest research, best practices, and emerging trends in education. Through a synthesis of personalized learning methodologies and a steadfast commitment to fostering a culture of collaboration and innovation, the academy sets out to revolutionize European education from its very core.

### 3.1 Concept and mission

In response to the urgent need to revitalize the appeal of the teaching profession across the European Union, as evidenced by concerning findings from the OECD's Teaching and Learning International Survey (TALIS) and compounded by the looming specter of a shortage of educators due to an aging workforce, a collaborative endeavor has been launched. This initiative, aligned with the overarching objectives outlined in the Call, unites 14 organizations from diverse backgrounds across nine countries to establish the Erasmus+ Teacher Academies Network. At its core, this network is driven by a profound mission to dynamically enhance teacher education by serving as a nexus for initial education providers, in-service training providers, and schools.

Central to this initiative is the unwavering commitment to elevate education policies and practices in Europe. By forging networks and communities of practice for teacher education providers, the Erasmus+ Teacher Academies Network seeks to foster a culture of collaboration and innovation. The aim is to converge pre-service and in-service providers, alongside key stakeholders such as teacher associations, ministries, and associate partners, to craft effective programs and strategies for professional learning that are not only accessible but also transferable across diverse educational landscapes.

To imbue a distinctly European dimension and internationalize teacher education, the initiative has birthed the STEAME Teacher Facilitators Academies. This visionary collaboration seeks to bridge gaps between teacher educators (HE professors) and schoolteachers from various European countries, envisioning the development of a blended initial training program. By facilitating the exchange of experiences and mutual support for the further development of teacher education in Europe, this collective effort addresses the critical priorities of the European Union. These include initiatives to promote digital literacy, sustainability, equity, and inclusion, with a strong emphasis on STEAME learning as the cornerstone of future project-based educational endeavors.

A pivotal aspect of this initiative is embodied in the Facilitators Academy, conceived as a vanguard in the reformation of teacher education across Europe. It endeavors to harness the potential of various forms of mobility, whether virtual, augmented, physical, or blended, to enrich the quality and accessibility of mentorship and practicum opportunities for educators. By embedding mobility as an integral component of teacher education provision across the continent, facilitated by the establishment of the European Federation of STEAME Teacher Academies and its accompanying Observatory, this collaborative effort aims to not only enhance the quality of teacher education but also to inform and influence policymakers at both the European and national levels.

Aligned with the four key interventions delineated in the OECD's Education 2030 report, including the implementation of innovative measurement mechanisms for Education 4.0 skills and the mainstreaming of technology-enhanced learning experiences, this initiative is positioned to make significant strides toward advancing teacher education and enriching the overall quality of education across Europe.

In essence, the concept and mission of the Erasmus+ Teacher Academies Network epitomize a comprehensive and concerted effort to confront the multifaceted challenges confronting the teaching profession in Europe. Through a blend of collaboration, innovation, and an unwavering dedication to excellence, this initiative aspires to cultivate a supportive ecosystem that empowers educators and enriches the educational experiences of students across the continent.

## 3.2 Key initiatives and strategies

In the dynamic realm of modern education, the STEAME-Academy project emerges as a beacon of transformative innovation, aiming to address the critical need to equip students with essential competencies for their future endeavors. Central to this initiative is the integration of STEAME activities into traditional education, ushering in a new era of immersive and interdisciplinary learning experiences.

Recognizing the pressing demand for a paradigm shift in educator training, the project endeavors to establish horizontal training programs at the university level. These programs are meticulously designed to equip future educators with the requisite skills and proficiency to craft engaging and effective curricula that resonate with the evolving needs of students in the twenty-first century.

Methodologically, the team aims to adopt a multifaceted approach, integrating instructional strategies such as experiential learning, collaborative projects, and immersive practicum experiences. Curriculum design is intended to be informed by pedagogical best practices, incorporating interdisciplinary approaches and real-world applications of STEAME principles. Assessment methods are planned to encompass both formative and summative evaluations, emphasizing authentic performance tasks and portfolios to gauge teacher proficiency. Moreover, innovative techniques like flipped classrooms and gamification are intended to be seamlessly integrated to enhance engagement and improve learning outcomes among educators.

Empirical evidence and case studies are envisioned to play a pivotal role in demonstrating the impact of our initiatives on educational outcomes. Quantitative data on student performance pre- and post-participation is expected to showcase improvements in academic achievement and critical thinking skills. Qualitative feedback from educators and students is anticipated to offer valuable insights into the perceived benefits of our interventions on teaching practices and student engagement. Comparative studies may further assess the effectiveness of our trained educators compared to those without similar training.

To establish robust feedback mechanisms, the team aims to involve educators, mentors, and administrators. Surveys, focus groups, and individual interviews conducted at regular intervals are planned to gather feedback from participants. Online platforms and discussion forums are expected to facilitate ongoing communication and collaboration, enabling real-time feedback and dialog. Systematic analysis of feedback is intended to inform program refinements and adaptations to better meet evolving stakeholder needs.

Incorporating findings from longitudinal studies or follow-up assessments is considered critical to understanding the sustained impact of our programs. Longitudinal data tracking the progress of educators and students over time is expected to provide insights into long-term effectiveness on professional development and educational achievement. These studies are envisioned to explore factors such as retention rates among our trained educators, changes in teaching practices over time, and student outcomes beyond immediate program participation.

Moreover, the project champions the pivotal role of teachers as mentors across Europe, facilitating the transfer of knowledge and expertise to nurture a new generation of educators adept at fostering innovation and critical thinking among students. Through a comprehensive Framework for Teacher Facilitator Proficiency, educators are empowered to cultivate a rich learning environment that seamlessly integrates STEAME principles into educational practices.

Furthermore, the establishment of STEAME Learning Modules serves as a cornerstone in this transformative journey, offering educators a diverse array of adaptable resources designed to enrich learning experiences across various educational contexts. These modules, grounded in a multidisciplinary approach, ignite curiosity and promote hands-on exploration, fostering a deeper understanding of complex concepts and real-world applications.

The project also endeavors to foster a culture of collaboration and knowledge exchange through the creation of an Observatory for International Sharing of Best Practices. By serving as a centralized hub for collecting and disseminating global insights and innovations in STEAME education, educators are empowered to leverage successful strategies and approaches to enrich their teaching practices.

In parallel, the creation of a dynamic online Community of Practice for Facilitators provides educators with a platform to connect, collaborate, and seek guidance from peers. Through forums, webinars, and collaborative projects, educators engage in ongoing professional development, sharing insights and success stories to advance STEAME education collectively.

Finally, the project culminates in the establishment of a robust Certification Program, recognizing educators' proficiency in STEAME facilitation. Transparent assessment criteria ensure rigor and credibility, while collaboration with education authorities ensures seamless integration into existing accreditation systems, further legitimizing educators' expertise in STEAME education.

Together, these initiatives underscore the STEAME-Academy project's commitment to equipping educators with the necessary skills and resources to navigate the complexities of modern education. By fostering collaboration, innovation, and continuous improvement, the project aims to catalyze a transformative shift in educational practices, ultimately enhancing the quality of teacher education and preparing students for success in an ever-evolving world.

### *3.2.1 Empowering educators: the Teacher Facilitators Competence Framework*

The Teacher Facilitators Competence Framework serves as a comprehensive guide, outlining the essential skills, knowledge, and proficiencies required for future STEAME teachers. Developed in collaboration with universities, pedagogical institutes, and educational authorities, this framework represents a collective effort to align teacher education with the demands of the twenty-first-century educational landscape.

Universities, pedagogical institutes, and educational authorities are provided with the Competence Framework to catalyze transformative changes in education systems and future schools. By integrating STEAME principles into university degree programs, educators are equipped with a blended learning provision that emphasizes STEAME teaching and learning facilitation. This proactive approach ensures that educators are prepared to meet the evolving needs of students and adapt to emerging trends in education.

The Competence Framework facilitates the seamless integration of STEAME pedagogy into existing educational practices, fostering a blended learning environment that combines traditional teaching methods with innovative STEAME approaches. By providing educators with the necessary tools and guidance, the framework empowers them to create dynamic learning experiences that engage students and foster critical thinking, creativity, and collaboration.

At its core, the Teacher Facilitators Competence Framework embodies a commitment to driving educational innovation and excellence. By equipping educators with the skills to effectively implement STEAME principles, the framework lays the foundation for transformative change within educational institutions. Through ongoing professional development and collaboration, educators are empowered to harness the power of STEAME education to inspire future generations of innovators and problem-solvers.

The Teacher Facilitators Competence Framework represents a pivotal step toward empowering educators and reshaping educational systems to meet the demands of the twenty-first century. By providing a roadmap for integrating STEAME principles into teaching practices, this framework equips educators with the tools and knowledge they need to prepare students for success in an increasingly complex and interconnected world. Through collaborative efforts and a shared commitment to excellence, the STEAME-Academy project aims to empower educators to lead the way toward a brighter future for education.

### *3.2.2 Enhancing collaboration: Community of Practice and Mentorship Programs*

In the dynamic landscape of modern education, collaboration among educators plays a pivotal role in fostering innovation, sharing best practices, and ultimately improving student outcomes. Recognizing the value of collaboration, the STEAME-Academy project has prioritized the establishment of a robust Community of Practice (CoP) and Mentorship Programs to empower educators across Europe.

*DOI: http://dx.doi.org/10.5772/intechopen.1004946*

The Community of Practice serves as a virtual platform where educators from diverse backgrounds can come together to share insights, exchange ideas, and collaborate on innovative approaches to teaching and learning. By leveraging the collective expertise and experiences of its members, the CoP provides a fertile ground for professional growth and development.

Within the CoP, educators have the opportunity to engage in meaningful discussions, participate in webinars and workshops, and contribute to collaborative projects. Through these interactions, they gain valuable perspectives, acquire new skills, and stay abreast of the latest trends and developments in STEAME education.

Moreover, the CoP fosters a sense of belonging and camaraderie among its members, creating a supportive ecosystem where educators feel empowered to take risks, experiment with new pedagogical approaches, and continually strive for excellence in their practice. This sense of community not only enriches the professional lives of educators but also enhances their overall job satisfaction and well-being.

In addition to the CoP, the STEAME-Academy project also offers Mentorship Programs designed to pair experienced educators with their less experienced counterparts. Through these mentorship relationships, mentees benefit from the guidance, support, and wisdom of their mentors, who provide valuable insights, share practical strategies, and offer personalized feedback to help mentees navigate the challenges of teaching.

Mentors serve as role models and sources of inspiration for mentees, helping them develop the confidence, skills, and resilience needed to excel in their roles as educators. By fostering a culture of mentorship, the STEAME-Academy project aims to cultivate a new generation of empowered and effective teachers who are equipped to meet the evolving needs of students in the twenty-first century.

In conclusion, the Community of Practice and Mentorship Programs established by the STEAME-Academy project are integral components of its broader mission to enhance collaboration and support among educators. By providing educators with opportunities to connect, learn, and grow together, these initiatives contribute to the overall quality of teacher education and ultimately benefit students by promoting excellence in teaching and learning.

## 4. Analyzing the impact: opportunities and challenges of STEAME teacher facilitators

In the ever-changing landscape of education, the imperative to equip teachers for the challenges and opportunities of tomorrow's world has reached unprecedented heights. At the brink of Education 3.0 and 4.0, characterized by the rapid integration of technological innovations and evolving societal needs, educators find themselves at the forefront of a transformative journey fraught with both obstacles and prospects.

Foremost among the challenges facing educators is the breakneck pace of technological advancement. Groundbreaking developments such as artificial intelligence, automation, and virtual reality are reshaping industries and labor markets, necessitating an adaptation of teaching methodologies to prepare students for a workforce that values ingenuity, critical thinking, and adaptability. The integration of STEM and arts education, encapsulated within the framework of STEAME, emerges not merely as an option but as an imperative in nurturing forward-thinking learners.

Moreover, the increasing interconnectedness of our global community presents educators with a myriad of challenges and opportunities. While it affords unparalleled access to knowledge and resources, it also requires that teachers navigate a diverse array of cultural perspectives and cultivate inclusive learning environments. Embracing diversity and instilling principles of global citizenship are thus pivotal in equipping students with the cross-cultural competencies necessary to thrive in an interconnected world.

The seismic impact of the COVID-19 pandemic has further underscored the importance of digital literacy and proficiency among educators. The rapid adoption of remote and hybrid learning models has accentuated the need for teachers to adeptly leverage technology in their pedagogical practices. Moving forward, educators must continue to explore innovative teaching methodologies and harness digital tools to augment student engagement and optimize learning outcomes in both physical and virtual learning environments.

Amidst these challenges, however, lie significant opportunities waiting to be seized. The emphasis on interdisciplinary learning, epitomized by STEAME education, offers a fertile ground for nurturing creativity, collaboration, and problem-solving skills among students. By seamlessly integrating science, technology, engineering, arts, mathematics, and entrepreneurship, educators can curate dynamic learning experiences that prepare students to navigate the multifaceted complexities of the modern world.

Furthermore, the growing recognition of the significance of social-emotional learning presents educators with a unique opportunity to foster empathy, resilience, and self-awareness in their students. Prioritizing holistic development not only equips students with the requisite skills for academic success but also empowers them to navigate life's challenges with confidence and compassion, ultimately cultivating a generation of empathetic and resilient individuals poised to shape a brighter future.

In essence, the evolving educational landscape presents both challenges and opportunities for educators. By embracing innovation, leveraging technology, and prioritizing holistic development, educators can effectively navigate these changes and prepare students to thrive in an ever-changing world.

## 5. Conclusions

In conclusion, the STEAME Teacher Facilitators Academy represents a beacon of innovation and progress in the dynamic landscape of modern education. Its visionary approach, unwavering commitment to excellence, and dedication to empowering educators make it poised to redefine the contours of teacher development and educational quality across Europe.

This chapter has explored the transformative potential inherent in multidisciplinary, project-based learning methodologies and the pivotal roles played by educators and aspiring teachers in shaping the educational landscape. The STEAME Teacher Facilitators Academy stands at the forefront of this transformative journey, an ambitious initiative aimed at revolutionizing educational landscapes into dynamic hubs of STEAME project-based learning.

By illuminating the conceptual framework, overarching objectives, and targeted solutions of the STEAME Teacher Facilitators Academy, the tapestry of this transformative endeavor has been unraveled. The academy strives to bridge critical gaps in teacher competence, tools, and methodologies, providing comprehensive training and support mechanisms to empower educators with the skills to orchestrate impactful learning experiences.

Central to the ethos of the STEAME Teacher Facilitators Academy is its commitment to delivering holistic solutions that address multifaceted challenges in education.

Through networking among educators, the STEAME Teacher Facilitators Academy fosters a culture of continuous improvement, pushing educators toward the forefront of educational innovation.

Upon reflection, it becomes clear that the visionary approach, innovative solutions, and collaborative ethos of the STEAME Teacher Facilitators Academy have the potential to redefine educational excellence throughout Europe. By embracing this initiative, educators and students alike are inspired to embark on a transformative journey toward a brighter future, where learning is not merely a process but a pathway to empowerment and lifelong success.

## Acknowledgements

This work was developed at the research group GILT from IPP/ISEP, with the support of FCT/MCTES (UIDB/05627/2020, UIDB/05627/2020, 950/2019) and STEAM - Project code: 101102619 — STEAME-ACADEMY. The authors acknowledge the use of ChatGPT for language polishing of the manuscript.

## Conflict of interest

The authors declare no conflict of interest.

## Author details

Paula Escudeiro[1*], Márcia Campos Gouveia[1], Nuno Escudeiro[1] and Francisca Escudeiro[2]

1 Games, Interaction and Learning Technologies (GILT), Polytechnic University of Porto (IPP), Porto, Portugal

2 School of Medicine and Biomedical Sciences (ICBAS), Porto University (UP), Porto, Portugal

*Address all correspondence to: pmo@isep.ipp.pt

## References

[1] Song Y, Martin-Hansen L, Akerson VL, Buck GA, Al-Balushi SM. STEM teacher education: An overview. In: Anderson J, Li Y, editors. Reforming Science Teacher Education Programs in the STEM Era. Cham: Palgrave Macmillan; 2023. pp. 1-16

[2] Thomas K, Huffman D. Challenges and Opportunities for Transforming from STEM to STEAM Education. Hershey, Pennsylvania: IGI Global; 2020

[3] Anderson J, Li Y, editors. Advances in STEM Education. College Station, TX, USA: Springer Nature Switzerland AG; 2020

[4] Ryoo J, Winkelmann K, editors. Innovative Learning Environments in STEM Higher Education: Opportunities, Challenges, and Looking Forward, SpringerBriefs in Statistics. Cham, Switzerland: Springer; 2021. DOI: 10.1007/978-3-030-58948-6

[5] Williams JM. Making Changes in STEM Education: The Change Maker's Toolkit. Boca Raton, Florida: CRC Press; 2023

[6] Burrows A, Borowczak M, Myers A, Schwortz A, McKim C. Integrated STEM for teacher professional learning and development: 'I need time for practice'. Education Sciences. 2021;**11**(1):21. DOI: 10.3390/educsci11010021

[7] Al-Balushi SM, Martin-Hansen L, Song Y, editors. Reforming Science Teacher Education Programs in the STEM Era: International and Comparative Perspectives, Palgrave Studies on Leadership and Learning in Teacher Education. Cham, Switzerland: Palgrave Macmillan; 2023. DOI: 10.1007/978-3-031-27334-6

[8] Geesa RL, Rose MA, Stith KM, editors. Leadership in Integrative STEM Education: Collaborative Strategies for Facilitating an Experiential and Student-Centered Culture. Lanham, Maryland: Rowman & Littlefield; 2022

[9] Fomunyam KG, editor. Theorizing STEM Education in the 21st Century. London, UK, London, United Kingdom: IntechOpen; 2020. DOI: 10.5772/intechopen.77870

[10] Khine MS, Areepattamannil S, editors. STEAM Education: Theory and Practice. Switzerland AG: Springer Nature; 2019. DOI: 10.1007/978-3-030-04003-1

[11] Kaya-Capocci S, Peters-Burton E, editors. Enhancing Entrepreneurial Mindsets Through STEM Education. Cham: Springer; 2023. DOI: 10.1007/978-3-031-17816-0

[12] Delahunty T, Ní Ríordáin M, editors. Perspectives in Contemporary STEM Education Research: Research Methodology and Design. Abingdon, Oxon: Routledge; 2022. ISBN: 9780367621360

[13] Johnson CC, Mohr-Schroeder MJ, Moore TJ, English LD, editors. Handbook of Research on STEM Education. New York: Routledge; 2020. ISBN: 9780367075620

[14] Wilson-Kennedy ZS, Byrd GS, Kennedy E, Frierson HT, editors. Broadening Participation in STEM: Effective Methods, Practices, and Programs, Diversity in Higher Education. Vol. 22. Bingley, UK: Emerald Publishing Limited; 2020. ISBN: 178756908X

[15] Allan CN, Campbell C, Crough J. Blended Learning Designs

in STEM Higher Education: Putting Learning First. Singapore: Springer; 2019. DOI: 10.1007/978-981-13-6982-7

[16] Schuck S, Aubusson P, Burden K, Brindley S. Uncertainty in Teacher Education Futures: Scenarios, Politics and STEM. Singapore: Springer; 2018. DOI: 10.1007/978-981-10-8246-7

[17] Barak M, Yuan S. A cultural perspective to project-based learning and the cultivation of innovative thinking. Thinking Skills and Creativity. 2021;**39**:100766. DOI: 10.1016/j.tsc.2020.100766

[18] Demir C, Önal N. The effect of technology-assisted and project-based learning approaches on students' attitudes towards mathematics and their academic achievement. Education and Information Technologies. 2021;**26**:3375-3397. DOI: 10.1007/s10639-020-10398-8